MW01037979

Loving the Addict in Your Pew: A roadmap for building a church-based recovery ministry by Charles Robinson III

Books may be purchased by contacting the publisher and author at:

Elements Behavioral Health
5000 E. Spring Street, Suite 650
Long Beach, CA 90815
www.elementsbehavioralhealth.com

Cover Design: Allison Liu

Editor: Meghan Vivo

First Edition

Printed in U.S.

Acknowledgments

There is a man who has been instrumental in my life –
Rick Pellow. Rick loaned me some money so I could begin an
independent life. I knew I couldn't pay him back. He said,
"Don't worry about paying me back; when an 18-year-old asks
you for help, you be there to help him." That is a debt that
won't be paid in full until I take my last breath.

I want to give thanks to God for my beautiful bride of 32 years,
Vicky Vineyard Robinson. Her delightful smile and genuine way
of taking life in stride is an example to me and many others. We
celebrate daily our finding of His purpose for our lives.

I want to thank God for our healthy sons, Chad, Colby, Conner
and Teyon, and our four beautiful daughters-in-laws. At the time
of this writing I have three wonderful grandchildren, one sweet
little girl and two rowdy little boys. They all mean the world to me.

I also want to acknowledge a lineage of men that have had an
influence on me: my granddad, Charles Watson Robinson Sr.,
M.D., and my dad, Charles Watson Robinson Jr., M.D. These
men taught me the importance of working hard and the need for
continued education. I am Charles Watson Robinson, III, and
my oldest son, Chad, is the fourth (IV) and his son, Charlie, is
the fifth (V). Fortunately, I have been able to know and see all
five generations of these men, and for that I'm truly grateful. To
my sweet mother, Shirley Gay Robinson, who introduced me to
this life I live today. I miss my mom and dad every day, and hope
I can leave a legacy as they have.

I want to thank Henderson Hills Baptist Church and its elder
board for seeing the need for a recovery ministry in our church.
They took a chance with me; they put time, money and energy
into a program that has changed many families' lives. I'm specifically
thankful to Dr. Dennis Newkirk, who taught me the importance
of the Word of God. About twenty years ago, he asked me what

my purpose was and shared that he felt that my purpose had to do with recovery. Because Dr. Newkirk, the elder board, the church and I said "yes," there is a thriving recovery ministry at Henderson Hills.

I would be remiss if I didn't acknowledge and thank David Sack, M.D., and the team at Elements Behavioral Health. Elements introduced me to Gary Gilles – without him, this book would have simply remained an idea or a dream.

Finally I want to thank the men in my life who have taken me under their wings. My sponsors, Wayne B., Johnie O., Paul P. & Tom B., my many mentors, but to name a few, David Wright, John Leadem, my dad and granddad, and the young man that I get to work with daily. If it wasn't for their example of serving, I wouldn't have understood the importance of sharing the gift that God has given me.

This world is a tough place to live, with constant bombardment from the evil forces. Those forces come in all shapes and sizes – to mention just a few, pornography, gambling, eating disorders and drug and alcohol addiction. Addictions/afflictions are nothing new; they are simply the "idols" of the day. Let the church house be a place where people can find solace from their hurts, hang-ups and habits, loving the addict in the pew.

Endorsements for Loving the Addict in Your Pew

Chuck Robinson offers this strategically helpful guide to church-based recovery ministry with the heart of a pastor, skills of a therapist and insights of one thoroughly accomplished in recovery ministry. Jesus is calling each of his churches to share his vision of "the harvest" to include reaching addicts and walking with them the whole journey to fully recovered lives. *Loving the Addict in Your Pew* will give you strategic assistance for fulfilling that mission.

– *T.C. Ryan, author of Ashamed No More*

Families on the hunt for resources to help their loved ones in active alcoholism and/or addiction are often confused about options and challenged by the lack of accessible care. This is also true for churches committed to providing resources for the needs of their community especially in the field of addiction. Addiction is an epidemic in our society and one of the most prevalent needs that pastors face – whether these problems are obvious or hidden by a deluge of "symptoms" of the affliction – like jail time, DUIs, broken relationships, under-employment and more. Chuck has written a book that makes sense out of the chaos of myth and ignorance associated with this subject. It's clear, practical and well-grounded. It should sit on every pastor's desk.

– *Teresa McBean, minister and executive director of Northstar Community and the National Association for Christian Recovery*

Ministries are often at a loss as to how to help those within their congregations who are struggling with alcohol and drug use. With this book, Charles Robinson creates a framework and a toolkit for building a recovery ministry that reaches out to those who so often go unsupported, helps them heal, and brings them back into the life of the church. It's a practical roadmap for understanding and dealing with addiction that never forgets the power of faith in changing lives.

– *Noted addictionologist David Sack, MD, chief medical officer of Elements Behavioral Health*

After working in the field of addiction recovery for the past thirty years, we have read a lot of material that helps people understand how to deal with addiction. Chuck has written a guide for people in general, but especially those inside our churches. Most churches don't know how to deal with addiction and tend to enable or often ignore the fact that there is a problem within their doors. We will refer people to Chuck's book so that they can better help those who suffer from these problems. The book reaches out to the Christian community as well as the recovery community. You have done a great job in putting something out there that makes sense and is easy to understand. Thank you for this guide that can help so many.
– Jim Riley, former Miami Dolphin and founder of Jim Riley Outreach non-profit ministry

Chuck offers a comprehensive guide from the trenches for pastors who long to touch their own members who are hurting with expansive love and therapeutic excellence.
– Sherry Young, PhD, CSAT, senior regional outreach director at Elements Behavioral Health

As the saying goes, "experience is the best teacher." And there is no person with greater experience building a recovery ministry inside the walls of the church than Chuck Robinson. Chuck is a pioneer, a visionary and a true servant of the broken-hearted. He knows what he is talking about and has given away this knowledge with this book. You will now have the great opportunity to tap into Chuck's experience, education and methodology and use it for the betterment of your flock.

If you are working with the addicted or anyone associated with them, I would strongly encourage you to immerse yourself in this book. It will help you give HOPE to others!
– Lance Lang, author and executive director of Hope is Alive

Chuck Robinson has journeyed a long way. He has traveled the road from addiction, to recovery, to ministry to those in addiction and recovery. Now he is providing a step-by-step pathway for the church to follow in order to help those who are caught in the trap of addiction. Recovery ministry is difficult, messy work, and the challenges and disappointments along the way are many. But the successes make the journey well worth the pain, effort, and time. The question really isn't if the church should minister to those who are caught in addition; it is how to most effectively use the time and resources available to do so. *Loving the Addict in Your Pew* is a valuable resource for churches and others. Chuck's many years of experience and honest, straightforward guidance will help you avoid many pitfalls and find success in building a Christian recovery ministry.

– Dr. Dennis Newkirk, senior pastor/teacher at Henderson Hills Baptist Church, Edmond, OK

Chuck Robinson and I have worked together and been friends for more than twenty years. My wife is a recovering alcoholic who from time to time relapsed. I was on the phone making arrangements for her return to treatment when a voice came to me and said, "Call Chuck Robinson." I did. Within hours she was on her way to Lucida Treatment Center in Florida. The treatment at and after Lucida were exactly what she and we needed. She will always be a recovering alcoholic. But, we now have the tools, which we use each day, to deal effectively with it and lead happy and productive lives.

From time to time, God sends angels into your life. They don't have wings and fly around. They are people like Chuck Robinson who give their lives so that others might live. Chuck Robinson is our angel, we love him and give thanks for him every day. Why did God tell me to call Chuck? I have no idea, but I will be forever grateful that He did. Listen to what God has to say through Chuck and he will be your angel as he is ours.

– David Wright, investment banker at First Liberties Financial in New York

"I actually thank God for my addiction." These words from a devoted Christian man I deeply respect caught me a bit off guard. I know that we are to be thankful for all things, knowing that God ultimately uses even the most painful things in life for our own good, but thankful for an addiction? This friend went on to explain that had it not been for his addiction, he likely would not have seen his need for Christ. While God certainly doesn't need to use an addiction to bring one to a point of recognizing our need for Him, it can be well-argued that those suffering from addictions, certainly those who have hit "rock bottom," are highly motivated to seek God and His healing presence in their lives.

In His "Mission Statement" found in Luke 4:18-19, Christ says that in addition to preaching the Gospel and providing "recovery of sight to the blind," He came to proclaim "release to the captives" and to "set free those who are downtrodden." What clearer mandate does the church need for starting a recovery ministry? And yet while the church should be the first place hurting people go for help, sadly it is often the last place hurting people go for help. Whether the cause be apathy, ignorance, judgmentalism or fear, the church at large has failed at large to be the "go to place" for those suffering from addictions, and hence has missed out on one of its greatest blessings – to see the power of God unleashed in the "downtrodden."

Thankfully one of God's choice servants has provided us with an insightful and practical guide on how the local church may rise up to the challenge of loving the addict in its pew. During my time at Henderson Hills Baptist Church as an active church member and later as a staff member serving as Executive Director for Ministries of Jesus, I saw God call a well-intentioned yet somewhat ill-equipped man to take on the challenge of establishing a recovery ministry at the church. And yet over a ten-year period I saw God at work in Chuck Robinson in amazing ways. He truly honored the heart of a man sold out for Christ, transforming him into an incredibly gifted leader who blessed the body of Christ at Henderson Hills by showing them the incredible blessing that falls on a church willing to love the addicted – those Christ loved and died for. My prayer is that this book will help usher in a new era of joyful and productive ministry for you and your church as you move out in faith, considering that He looks not on your ability but rather on your availability.

Rise up, O men of God!
Have done with lesser things.
Give heart and mind and soul and strength
To serve the King of kings.
Rise up, O men of God!
The kingdom tarries long.
Bring in the day of brotherhood
And end the night of wrong.
Rise up, O men of God!
The church for you doth wait,
Her strength unequal to her task;
Rise up and make her great!
Lift high the cross of Christ!
Tread where His feet have trod.
As brothers of the Son of Man,
Rise up, O men of God!
"Rise Up O Men of God," William Pierson Merrill

About the Author

Chuck Robinson served as the first pastor of recovery at Henderson Hills Baptist Church in Edmond, Oklahoma. He is a licensed minister, a licensed alcohol and drug counselor, and a certified sex addiction therapist. Today, he works as the national director of Christian programming and outreach with Elements Behavioral Health, a nationwide network of addiction and mental health treatment centers, where he oversees the Three Strands^{SM} Christian addiction treatment program at select facilities. Robinson holds a bachelor's degree in business management and a master's degree in substance abuse studies from the University of Central Oklahoma. In personal recovery from addiction since 1982, Robinson has happily celebrated 32 years of marriage and has four sons and three grandchildren.

Table of Contents

Introduction

Do you know this man?

Jerry has a secret that only his wife knows and she would never tell. There's too much at stake. Actually, Jerry has several secrets. And he's good at hiding them. He's so good, in fact, that he almost believes the façade he portrays to everyone. He's a family man who runs a successful business, volunteers on several committees and serves as an elder in his church. He's well-respected in the community and routinely sought out for counsel by members of his church.

But despite all of the good things Jerry does he's haunted by his secrets: past and present. Raised in a home with an alcoholic father that he could never please, Jerry became an overachiever. He thought that straight A's or being captain of the sports team would win his father's elusive approval. It never did. In high school, as a way to cope with the perpetual feeling of never measuring up, Jerry started drinking. At first, it was only when socializing with friends. But, by the time he was in college, he was drinking daily and often alone. He would quit drinking for periods of time but always returned to alcohol when life stressors were too difficult to manage on his own. He married soon after college, had three children, started his own business and by all external measures was "successful." But, he continued to drink and over time added illicit drugs and pornography to his list of coping methods.

Now, well into mid-life, he outwardly appears to have it all together. But privately he feels the burden of the double life he hides from everyone outside his family. He still drinks on a daily basis, occasionally does drugs (marijuana and cocaine) and compulsively engages with pornography that has led to at least one online affair with an anonymous woman. There's a part of him that wants to shed this façade and come clean but he fears humiliating his family, losing respect at work and suffering through the shame of being removed as a leader in his church.

Jerry feels an acute tension between his desired life and the compulsive addictions that hold him captive. Yet, it never occurs to him to look for help in the most obvious place: his church. In fact, the church community is where he fears the greatest rejection were his secrets to become known. But, how might it be different for Jerry if his church openly invited people with addictions to seek help through a variety of services they offered on-site? Would he be more likely to get help and experience less shame? Would his family feel supported instead of humiliated? I believe the answer to these questions is a resounding "yes."

As you will see in the pages that follow, there are many people like Jerry in your congregation who have addiction-related secrets. We need to be careful to not judge those who struggle or buy into the myth that addiction is not a problem in my church. People struggling with addictions are in every church. They long to have a safe place to tell their story to someone who cares and be freed from the compulsive behaviors that imprison them. How do I know that? I used to be one of them.

My journey toward healing
I started experimenting with drugs and alcohol in high school. I thought that smoking marijuana, taking pills and getting drunk gave me a type of peer acceptance I couldn't find anywhere else. But, what started out as a way of "being cool" quickly took on a life of its own. In college I was beginning to live with the real-world consequences of my strengthening addiction. I got kicked out of the dorm, held up at gunpoint because of drugs, went to jail for possession of marijuana and drunkenness and flunked out of school. My life was swirling in a downward spiral. Yet, despite these and many other consequences, I continued using drugs and alcohol. I went through intensive treatment in December of 1980 and lived the roller-coaster of repeated relapse for about 16 months. Though I was attending a 12-step program

for alcoholism I couldn't make a complete break with my other drug of choice: cocaine.

It was about this time in my life that I met Vicky. We met on a flight to Wyoming that we were both taking for different business trips. I soon learned that Vicky too had substance use problems. She was addicted to alcohol. And, as often happens with substance abusers, the dysfunctional pull of our addictions caused us to feel an instant bond with each other. Our relationship moved quickly and a year later we were married.

The turning point in my life came one night after finishing some cocaine. Typically cocaine brings on a sense of extreme joy. But that night it had the opposite effect. It put me into a scary spin that I couldn't handle. I frantically began calling friends asking them to give me something to bring me down. I began reflecting on how miserable my life had become; how I had lost friends and jobs, racked up a police record, abused my body, squandered my opportunity to get a degree and wasted untold amounts of money on my addiction. I had accomplished nothing up to that point in my life that would help me become a responsible adult. Yet, according to some, these youthful years were supposed to be the best years of my life. As I fought through the terror of that night I had a rare moment of mental clarity: for the first time, I was able to admit that I was a drug addict and an alcoholic and I needed help.

Two days later, on Easter Sunday in fact, I reached out for help. I knew from my church background that Easter was the most sacred day of the year for Christians. It represented Christ's resurrection from the dead and God's promise of eternal life. I wanted – I needed – a new beginning. But, without help, I was destined to continue in my self-destructive ways. It was my mother who actually introduced me to recovery. She had gotten sober from her long-term addiction to alcohol just three years earlier and now I could see that I desperately needed help. Within a short time I attended my first recovery meeting and made a decision to turn my life around. I was ready to let God help me start a new chapter of my life.

Between the time of meeting and marrying, Vicky and I both knew we needed help. We weren't mature enough to understand that it was our addictive behavior that was the root of our relational problems: past and present. All we knew for certain was that we needed God to intervene and rescue us from ourselves. He provided this rescue largely through the relentless support of our 12-step group member, friends and pastors who rallied around us through many difficult situations. It was this accountability that eventually enabled us both to finally break free of addiction's death grip on our lives. My first day of sobriety was Tuesday, April 13, 1982 and Vicky's was shortly thereafter on June 3, 1982. Although there have been many tough days since that watershed commitment so many years ago, neither of us has broken our sobriety. I am grateful and humbled to say that God has enabled me to remain sober from drugs and alcohol for all of those years. But, it never would have been possible without the love, support, prayers and sacrifice of so many people in my and Vicky's life for the past three decades. As a way to give back for all that I've been given, I now devote most of my waking hours to helping others break the bonds of addiction and find hope through recovery.

I could not have written this book without my own experience of recovery. My recovery journey, with its many ups and downs, gives me great empathy for the millions of people in our church communities who are secretly engaged in a life-and-death struggle with their addictions. I have personally talked to thousands of people in need of recovery in my eight years as the first director of recovery for Henderson Hills Baptist Church in Edmond, Oklahoma (my home church) and more recently as National Director of Christian Programing & Outreach at Elements Behavioral Health. I now crisscross the country on a weekly basis speaking to church and community groups and consulting with pastors and counselors about the desperate need we have for a faith-based recovery ministry in local churches.

In that work, I've come to see that when it comes to addiction the church has a critical, often untapped role to play. People are desperately looking to the church for help, and the church is uniquely positioned to provide assistance. I have a passion for equipping churches across the country to disciple recovering addicts and their families. That discipleship should include:

- making an educated assessment of the person's addictive tendencies

- helping addicts find the treatment resources best suited to their needs

- tracking with them through the treatment process

- emotionally supporting family members of the addict, and

- ongoing follow-up with the addict and family after they leave treatment

We need to provide assistance to people with addictions through what I call a full-continuum of care. Later in the book I'll go into great detail of how this type of recovery ministry is created in the local church. But, for now, let me simply say anything less than a full-continuum of care is potentially setting addicts up for repeated failure. Getting clean and staying sober while in treatment are critically important to recovery but staying sober for the rest of life requires a great deal of support, guidance and accountability. It can be an arduous process. That's why in recovery we repeatedly say that we take it "one day at a time." If we lean too far out into the future we can easily be overwhelmed. We focus mainly on making sound and healthy decisions for today. But, we also need to plan for what's ahead. It is after treatment, when the addict is most prone to relapse, that the church can provide the most potent help by coming alongside the person in recovery through this process of discipleship. And that's where you come into the picture.

How this book can benefit you and your church
What would it look like for your church to be a healing and recovery-friendly community of people who understand addiction and want to help those trying to rebuild their lives? How would being that sort of church change your congregation and the larger community? I can tell you from personal experience that being a church that intentionally invites those with addictions to come for assistance will bring people into your midst that would never come otherwise. It is an enormous opportunity to transform lives: both body and soul.

Jesus was asked by the religious leaders of that time why he and his disciples were associating with sinners. It didn't make sense to them that Jesus would intentionally spend time with the social outcasts of that era, such as thieves, prostitutes and those who were chronically ill. Jesus responded by saying that it was "not those who are healthy who need a physician, but those who are sick" (Matthew 9:10-13; see also Luke 4:18). Jesus came to heal the sick, reach sinners and release those who are captive. The church needs to be a place of compassion where the sick, the downcast and those held captive by their addictions can find hope, reliable resources and competent care.

The main problem is that most churches don't have a strategy for how they can help addicts. Church leaders typically want to help those bound by addiction but usually just direct them to a nearby treatment center and/or local support group. I'm advocating that we delve further, much further into the recovery process with these individuals and families. But to do this we need a well-thought-out plan and a sound strategy. This book will lay out that strategy starting in chapter 2, by helping you to develop a model for addiction recovery. Once you are clear on how you view addiction, the road to recovery becomes doable. Perhaps the most important piece of the strategy is the decision each church must make about how much staff time and training they will allocate to equipping someone to facilitate the recovery ministry. This will be our focus in chapter 3. Ideally, a full-time dedicated staff position is optimal but not realistic for many churches. We'll look at roles and responsibilities of the recovery pastor from both full and part-time angles. Regardless of the staff time allocated for a recovery ministry, one essential responsibility of the person in this position is to continually network with local and national resources. In chapter 4 we'll walk through the type of resources that the recovery pastor must have to be an educated and resourceful referral agent. This extensive networking will also help in screening effective treatment centers from less effective ones. I'll provide some screening criteria for this task. Another critical skill of the recovery pastor is the ability to accurately assess addictive behaviors. There are specific tools and procedures that we will explore in chapter 5 that will help equip you for doing these screenings. An accurate screening is absolutely essential in order to make a targeted referral best suited to the individual in need. In chapter 6 we'll discuss what happens after the initial screening is made and the actual treatment begins. How is treatment supposed to progress? How can you support the addict in treatment and the family at the same time? This support of the addict and family requires education about abstinence, relational boundaries, co-dependence and self-care. We'll touch on how to educate the family on these areas and others in chapter 7. But, all of this people-helping on the part of the recovery pastor can result in a wounded healer if you do not practice your own ongoing self-care. In chapter 8, we'll discuss ways to stay fresh, keep your relational boundaries healthy and avoid compassion fatigue. In chapter 9, we discuss practical ways to make the recovery ministry work effectively in a church environment. These include how to help your congregation be supportive of a recovery ministry and ways to manage common problems that arise. We end with a hearty list of resources that you can draw upon for further study and inspiration. So, let's get started.

Chapter 1: Stories of transformation

Developing the recovery ministry from scratch

My story of transformation from addiction to sobriety began over three decades ago. But, over time God was clearly guiding me to achieve more from my transformation than personal abstinence from alcohol and drugs. I believe He was calling me to recovery work (Ephesians 2:10) and allowing me to use my journey and the many lessons learned along the way to help others. It all started when the pastor of my home church, Dr. Dennis Newkirk, preached a sermon series on the 12 steps and how the 12 steps can be seen from a biblical perspective as originating from Jesus' Sermon on the Mount and the book of James. The 12 steps are a set of guiding principles that outline a course of action for overcoming addictions. They originated with Alcoholics Anonymous (AA) but have been used as a tool for recovery in virtually all addictive behaviors. That series of sermons started a conversation between me and others on the pastoral staff that gradually evolved into my position as the first full-time director of recovery at Henderson Hills Baptist Church in Edmond, Oklahoma.

On the first day of my new job, I arrived at 8 a.m. with boxes of books and other items for my office. After unpacking everything, I sat at my desk and said, "Okay God, now what do I do?" Being the first to hold this position, I had no map to follow or defined job description. Yet, I had a purpose: to see people in our congregation saved from their addictions. I had no idea where our efforts would lead. I simply knew that God was calling me to help others be freed from their bondage to addictive behaviors.

In those early days as director of recovery in our church I reached out to a man who proved to be very helpful to me. His name was Jim Riley, founder of Jim Riley Outreach in Edmond, Oklahoma. When I called him I said, "Jim, you don't know me but I've been given this job as director of recovery for our church and I don't know where to start and what the resources for recovery are in our community." Without missing a beat Jim said, "Clear one day of your schedule this week for us to meet." I said, "Every day is clear Jim, pick one." So two days later Jim picked me up early and we spent the entire day driving from one treatment center to the next in a fairly large geographic radius of the church. Though this was a great way to help me get to know the local resources, I've since learned that it is sometimes necessary to go outside the local community to find the right treatment for a given individual. However, I needed to start somewhere and Jim introduced me to the people he knew at these local facilities. This helped me see the critical need to build relationships with the recovery programs that we might be referring people to from our congregation. As you will see later in the book, that lesson has become one of the bedrock principles of building a successful recovery ministry in the local church. It worked very well for us and it will for you as well.

As I moved forward in my new position, there were plenty of mistakes. But, despite the steep learning curve we decided as a church to take a bold stance and publicly invite those struggling with addictions to ask us for help. Our thinking was: now that we had a full-time director of recovery we could better meet the needs of this population. Yet, people didn't know how to respond at first. They weren't accustomed to our church, or any church for that matter, openly encouraging those with addictions to reach out to church staff. There was uncertainty among many in the congregation. Would they be rejected, shamed or humiliated if they told their secrets? The only way to find out was to make the path to recovery as safe and affirming as possible. Gradually, individuals began to contact me, telling me their story and pleading for help. Those early days of having little to do were quickly replaced with not enough hours in the day as people began to see that our recovery ministry was truly meeting some important needs.

What started out as a vague directive from the church leaders to "create a recovery ministry" eventually blossomed into a ministry well beyond our expectations. For example, we had the largest adult education class in the church, entirely made up of people in recovery. We met on Saturday nights. We emotionally supported addicts and their families in their journey toward healing throughout the whole process of recovery, from screening to aftercare. We had two sober living homes, one male and one female, that have now evolved into an apartment complex for men that supports their recovery after residential treatment. We had a thriving Celebrate Recovery (CR)* aftercare program in place with many involved on a regular basis. We made a decision early on that our recovery ministry would treat both the body and soul. So, every person in the recovery house was also required to attend church, daily AA meetings and a weekly Celebrate Recovery meeting that included a CR Step Study. We were not interested in just helping them to achieve sobriety, we wanted them to have a relationship with Jesus Christ and walk the road of recovery by relying on the power of the Holy Spirit to give them strength, courage and discipline.

Stories of transformation

Helping others to recover from their addictions is now my life's calling. The one word that best characterizes my work in the recovery ministry is transformation. The definition of the term transformation is to make a thorough or dramatic change. I am passionate about seeing addicts and their family's lives transformed from the inside out. When I think of transformation, Romans 12:2 comes to mind: "Do not be conformed to this world, but be transformed by the renewal of your mind, that by testing you may discern what is the will of God, what is good and acceptable and perfect." This transformation of the mind, body and soul takes time, patience and an educated approach to addiction recovery. The church is in a prime position to step into that role with the proper preparation.

Over the years I have walked the recovery path with many people attempting to break free from their addictions. In just the eight years I was director of recovery at Henderson Hills I had the privilege of referring more than 200 addicts to various treatment programs. Fortunately, I have many more recovery success stories than recovery failures. While I thank God for every person whom I have helped escape from the clutches of addiction, there are those that didn't make it for one reason or another and they stick in my memory like a thorn that I can't extract. When addiction takes the life of someone, especially someone I know, it hits me hard. In fact, attempting to prevent that loss of life is what gets me out of bed every morning and motivates me to continue this work and get churches involved along the way.

There are many stories but one in particular that I would like to tell will forever fuel my passion for helping others. Perhaps it will touch you as well. I've changed some of the details to protect the privacy of the individuals involved, but the story is true.

Ethan's story

Ethan was a gentle-spirited guy I met during my time as director of recovery at Henderson Hills. His aunt is actually the one who first made contact with me saying her nephew needed help because he had a host of addictions that included drugs, alcohol and sex. As I got to know him I instantly liked him. He was articulate, a natural leader and had a servant's heart. He previously served in law enforcement and at the peak of his career had achieved a respectable rank and been highly decorated. But, his addictions caused one unfortunate consequence after the other eventually ending in him being released from the police department.

When I met Ethan he had just completed inpatient treatment and was looking for a place to live to help transition back into daily life. His family was not yet ready for him to come back home so I found him a place in our recovery house. Within a short time, I made Ethan the manager of the recovery house. He was doing well, attending meetings and working the program as well as could be expected. This progress went on for some time before he started to crash.

One day he left the recovery house with no advance notice and wouldn't answer his phone. No one knew where he was. After an extensive search we found him at a nearby park just as he was attempting to cut his wrists. It was my first experience with a suicide attempt. We were able to get him the medical and psychiatric help he needed at the time to stabilize him. While he was hospitalized, he was diagnosed as having a bipolar condition. This was the beginning of a long journey that unfortunately had a sad ending.

To get Ethan the ongoing help he needed, we found a therapeutic community some distance away that seemed to fit his needs and would require an extended stay. He agreed to go and did well in their program and even took on leadership roles while there. But, the cloud of depression never completely lifted from him. He didn't seem to have any joy.

After this round of treatment he came back to our recovery house and was doing well. A couple of months had passed and he had worked his way back to being one of our leaders. Things appeared to be going well, when seemingly out of nowhere he relapsed. This relapse led to a series of consequences that he apparently found too difficult to deal with and shortly thereafter ended his life.

Ethan's death affected me deeply. It was then that I made a promise to myself that his death would not be in vain. This quest to keep addiction from taking lives, breaking up families, traumatizing children, and eroding the social fabric of our society is a driving force in my life. Addiction treatment centers play an important part in the recovery process but the church is even better positioned to help people with addictions when there is a community of people willing to help at all stages of recovery. We can't save everyone, as is evident by Ethan's story, but we can do so much more than we are currently doing.

Whether you realize it or not, there are people like Ethan in your congregation. Some of these people will never tell their secret until they feel safe enough to do so. Why not consider how you can begin to make this happen in your church.

In chapter three we will begin to put the pieces in place to help you understand what a recovery ministry could look like in your church. But first, we must start by building a working model of addiction.

* Celebrate Recovery is a Christ-based approach to recovery originally founded at Saddleback Church in Lake Forest, California.

Chapter 2: Building a working model of addiction

To most people it would seem logical to begin building a workable model of addiction by first defining the term addiction. Unfortunately, it's not that easy. Addiction is one of those words we use frequently to describe the behavior of someone who excessively uses one or more substances or compulsively engages in an activity, such as sex, gambling or shopping. And, while this general definition is adequate for daily conversation, it falls short of being specific enough for those who are interested in helping people recover from these problematic behaviors. So, here's the challenge: we first need to determine our working model of addiction before we can provide a clear definition. In other words, how we view addictive behavior shapes our definition and ultimately how we go about helping people recover. It may appear that we're putting the cart before the horse but you'll soon see why we must do it this way.

Though we can trace the misuse of substances such as alcohol as far back as we choose to go in American history, it is only in recent decades that the nature of addiction has been so hotly debated. Even today, the battle lines are often drawn between three broad and very diverse perspectives that attempt to explain the nature of addictive behavior. We'll take a closer look at each one. I'll then propose a fourth model that I think best captures the essence of those three models and sets us on firm ground to build a working model of addiction in the church.

The moral model
According to the moral model, addiction is the result of a moral failure to do what is right. From a societal perspective we could broadly say that behavior that reflects responsibility, moderation, consideration of others and reasonable self-care would qualify as appropriate or "right" behavior. In contrast, behavior that is self-indulgent, irresponsible, lacks the consideration of others and is excessive could be called "wrong" or failing to meet the minimum

standards of a common moral code.

The moral model of addiction assumes that we all have the ability to freely choose the behaviors we participate in. So those who abuse alcohol, use drugs or engage in compulsive behaviors, such as ongoing gambling, choose to do so. Addiction then is a logical consequence for the behaviors that a person chooses to engage in.

When addiction is seen through the lens of moral choices, it then seems common sense to "treat" the problem with a punitive response. For example, if a person is caught driving with a blood alcohol level above the legal limit, then he or she is given a citation. If it occurs more than once that person may face additional "punishment" with mandatory classes, loss of their driver's license or possibly jail time. Punishments for these and other addiction-related behaviors are designed to instill motivation in people to change and make better choices.

But it is not only the criminal justice system that approaches addiction from the moral model. The church is also a major proponent of this approach. Although most pastors or congregants could not explain the moral model in fine detail, most would assume that any behavior falling into the common description of "addiction" would reflect a series of poor or even immoral decisions. The church may or may not impose punishment for the choices that lead to addiction. But they most likely believe that the person can repent and turn their life around by making choices to stop the addictive behavior and find their moral bearings.

Possible strengths of the moral model
There are positive and negative aspects to the moral model. One positive is that this approach is straightforward, easy to understand and clear. There is no need to understand psychology, the inner workings of brain chemistry or an involved philosophy of motivation and behavioral change. It simply boils down to facing the consequences of your own choices.

Another positive aspect of the moral model is that it can heighten awareness of personal sin: how the person has hurt others, turned from God and made a mess of their life. Sin, in its basic definition, is knowing what is right but choosing not to do it. When people feel as though they've lost their moral bearings and have hit bottom, it can bring them to a place where they see their need for a Savior. I've seen many people reach this point in my recovery work over the years.

Possible weaknesses of the moral model

But, there are also some potential downsides to the moral model. First, we have a lot of research that points to a more complex origin of addiction beyond having a broken moral compass that leads to poor choices. For example, the National Institute on Drug Abuse (NIDA) says that "…genetic factors account for between 40 and 60 percent of a person's vulnerability to addiction; this includes the effects of environmental factors on the function and expression of a person's genes. A person's stage of development and other medical conditions they may have are also factors" (NIDA, 2013). In fact, there may be many biological, psychological and social factors that contribute to addictive tendencies that make simple choices more difficult or relapse more likely.

Another negative that specifically applies to the church is the perception of moral failure and the resulting shame that is experienced by the person trapped in their addiction. When we assume that a person can simply turn away from their addictive tendencies by making better choices, it is very easy to conclude that their inability to do so is a result of weak faith or lack of commitment to turn their life around. This perception of moral failure can breed judgment and criticism from others instead of support and encouragement. It can also foster feelings of shame in the person struggling with addiction because they feel as though they have failed themselves and others.

I think of a man I'll call "Ned" to illustrate how this burden of shame can negatively affect a person. Ned attended a neighboring church in our community but reached out to me because he knew we had a recovery ministry in our church. By the time we talked, he had already been through a couple of treatment programs for his alcoholism. He had seen periods of sobriety but relapsed each time. He was actively drinking again. His church was initially very supportive of his efforts to stay sober. But, with each relapse the leadership seemed to distance themselves from him as if they were giving up hope that he might be able to maintain his sobriety. The week before he came to see me his pastor had invited Ned to breakfast to tell him that he needed to make a choice: either get back into a treatment program or he was no longer welcome to be part of their congregation. Now, I don't believe this pastor was giving him an ultimatum to punish him but rather to motivate him to seek help. But, Ned interpreted this ultimatum as validation of his moral failure. He felt so much shame he no longer felt he could go back to his church, even if he were to engage in another round of treatment. This shame, which is so common among substance abusers, leaves a person feeling defective and often undermines motivation for getting the necessary treatment. This story about Ned is a perfect example of why the church needs to have a system in place for how to manage addiction at all levels of the treatment process; not simply after they complete a formal treatment program.

The disease model

According to the disease model, addiction is the result of an underlying disease that stems from altered brain functioning that makes a person susceptible to excessive types of behavior. Many who adopt a disease perspective also believe that genetics play an important part. It is the altered brain chemistry and genetic predisposition of some individuals that make them particularly vulnerable to abusing substances or engaging in compulsive activities once they are exposed to them. A person in the grip of addiction is considered a victim to the disease much like one who is diagnosed with cancer. It is not a chosen path or a result of irresponsible behavior. The person is robbed of their personal control over the illness and must seek treatment to learn to manage the ongoing disease.

Treatment typically involves a combination of medical intervention, patient education regarding the progression of addiction and individual and group counseling. But, it is important to understand that the disease model views addiction as an ongoing condition, even after recovery. You may be abstinent today, but you are vulnerable to relapse if you don't continue to respect the disease and the power it potentially has to alter the course of your life.

The disease model is supported by the medical profession, in part because this is in line with their training. The recovery industry largely supports this model as well, which includes those in various 12-step programs such as Alcoholics Anonymous (AA), Narcotics Anonymous (NA) and many others.

Possible strengths of the disease model
First, the disease model removes the moral factor from the addictive behavior. As a result, the scorn and shame that some addicts might experience under the moral model are replaced with compassionate care and medical intervention in the disease model. The addicted individual has an illness that they cannot control on their own and needs the assistance of others to help them manage it.

Another advantage of this approach is that because addiction is viewed as an illness, society is more willing to allocate resources to help those who have this disease. Whether those resources come from family, friends, the church, or the recovery or medical communities, there is more empathy for the person struggling with addiction than those perceived from the moral model where irresponsible choices are seen as the source of the problem.

A third positive contribution is that this model holds an unwavering commitment to abstinence as the goal of treatment and sobriety as a way of life. As rigid as some perceive this approach to be, it has helped literally hundreds of thousands (if not millions) of people to manage their addictions, heal broken relationships and live productive and healthy lives.

Possible weaknesses of the disease model

First, some of the ideas that have long been a part of the disease model, such as the progressive nature of the disease and subsequent loss of control, are seen by some in the research community as more anecdotal in nature and not based on hard science. Some studies have shown that alcoholics, for example, can exercise more control over the amount of alcohol they consume based upon the rewards and punishments that may exist (Frontiers in Psychiatry, 2013; 4:36).

Another criticism of the disease model is that it doesn't give much consideration to psychosocial factors, such as early life trauma or exposure to negative role models as contributors to the compulsive behavior that characterizes addiction.

The learning model

The third main approach that attempts to explain addictive behavior is the learning model. One way addictive behavior can be learned is by observing the behavior of others and following their lead. For example, a young adult who is socially awkward is hungry to make friends and falls in with a group his age that make alcohol and drug use a regular part of their social time together. He notices how relationally comfortable these people seem to be when they are drinking and using drugs. He wants to feel this same social confidence so he begins drinking excessively when with them. He notices a significant decline in his social anxiety when drinking and eagerly embraces this habit as part of his personal life.

This model also says you can learn addictive behavior by pairing certain activities with substance use. For example, as a way to cope with the daily stress of his traveling sales job, a middle-aged man occasionally smokes marijuana in his car between appointments. But, over time, he begins to associate being in the car with smoking marijuana and eventually gets a craving to smoke every time he gets in the car.

Another form of learning is by reinforcing and rewarding a behavior. For example, when a person finds it difficult to be sexually intimate with their spouse but is aroused by viewing pornography, regular engagement with pornography is likely to reoccur. The "reward" is sexual arousal. The more the person seeks the reward, the more it is reinforced and develops into compulsive behavior.

Addiction recovery from a learning perspective requires new ways of coping with stress. This might include finding new social circles with people who enjoy life without alcohol or drugs. Here is where 12-step support groups like AA, NA or Celebrate Recovery (CR) can be of immense help. Recovery could also involve working with a mental health therapist in either an inpatient or an outpatient setting to help unlearn unhealthy associations or misplaced reinforcements that might have been learned over time. This therapeutic work would also include developing effective ways to cope with life challenges in a more direct and effective manner.

Possible strengths of the learning model
The learning model approaches addiction recovery with the mindset that unhealthy patterns can be unlearned or corrected. It requires that a person modify their lifestyle as well as change social conditions that may be problematic. The therapeutic methods typically used to break unhelpful learned behaviors are cognitive behavioral therapy and/or behavioral therapy. Cognitive behavioral therapy works from the idea that if you change how you think you can change your behavior. For example, a person who is continually struggling with feelings of shame could begin to rework their distorted thoughts to find a new sense of worth

and value as someone created in God's image. Behavior therapy is focused on eliminating harmful behaviors by replacing them with constructive ones. For example, say a person repeatedly relapses when they hang out with old substance-using buddies. A behavioral approach would attempt to help them break out of that pattern and find new social networks of friends that will support their recovery. These approaches can often be found in many, if not most, of the recovery centers across the country.

Possible weaknesses of the learning model
Some critics of the learning model say that unlearning destructive habits and replacing them with adaptive learning is a good start but limited. Most of the emphasis is on changing unwanted behavior without delving into the psychology behind addiction, such as a person's motives for substance use, the development of self-esteem, or how past trauma may play a part in the evolution of addictive behaviors.

The biopsychosocial model
The fourth model, and the one that I will suggest as the preferred approach, is the biopsychosocial model of addiction. The biopsychosocial perspective has gotten a lot of attention in the last couple of decades. In fact, most addiction specialists now adopt some version of the biopsychosocial model over the other three already discussed. They don't necessarily outright reject the ideas presented in the disease, moral or learning models. Instead, the biopsychosocial approach extracts aspects from each of those three approaches to create a more comprehensive and diverse model that better explains ways addiction develops and how key factors (biological, psychological and social) interact in a person's life to influence the behavior of the addicted person. Let's break it down a little more so you can see the specific components.

Biological
The biological factors include both a genetic predisposition to develop an addiction and also how the ongoing use of substances

and addictive behavior affects the brain and body.

Psychological
The psychological factors are related to a person's behaviors, thoughts and feelings as they relate to their addiction. In recent years we've discovered that there are important links between addiction and mental health issues such as depression, anxiety, early trauma and certain personality characteristics.

Social
The social factors of addiction include the influence of family, friends, social groups (church, community involvement, civic organizations) that we regularly interact with and the larger culture (societal norms, media, and current trends).

Spiritual
I include the spiritual dimension in the biopsychosocial approach, as do many in the addiction recovery field. In fact, I believe there is a strong spiritual component to addiction. Whether a person realizes it or not, they are created in God's image (Genesis 1:26-7) and as a result they have a space inside them that can only be filled through a personal relationship with Him. When they turn away from their Creator and seek to fill that God-ordained place inside them with drugs, alcohol, sexual behavior, money, or possessions, they not only experience the natural biological, psychological and social consequences, but also a spiritual poverty that leaves their life void of meaning and purpose.

When you combine all four elements, it gives us a holistic picture of what a person needs in order to be healthy and how to structure addiction recovery in a way that addresses all of the important areas.

Biopsychosocial pathways to addiction
One strong advantage of the biopsychosocial model is that it allows for several pathways toward the development of addiction. Some embracing this model take the perspective that addiction is

a brain disease, meaning that prolonged use of substances alters brain circuits creating cravings, motivation and memory problems. These brain changes combined with a genetic predisposition and family history of substance use could represent one or more pathways. Others may cross over into addiction because of their inability to cope with overwhelming stress and use substances to numb their pain. Others may be subject to strong social influences, such as family dysfunction or living in a drug-infested environment that significantly contribute to their addiction. Or, there may be any combination of these factors working together. While the term "disease" can still be applied in this model, it does not imply that people caught in addiction are exempt from making healthy choices to recover or remain sober.

Definition of addiction

So, if we use the biopsychosocial model as the foundation for how we approach addictive behaviors, a working definition of addiction could be:

Addiction is an ongoing affliction that affects the brain's reward system, motivation, learning and memory. Altered brain function in these areas, due to prolonged use of substances, leads to biological, psychological, social and spiritual consequences.

Treatment using the biopsychosocial approach then should address all four components:

- Biological health includes sobriety but also physical health and sound lifestyle habits

- Psychological and emotional health is where the person learns how to manage their emotions and urges without masking them or numbing themselves with substances or other addictive behaviors

- Social health is choosing to be in relationship with people who support their recovery and who are seeking to be healthy individuals themselves

- Spiritual health requires that a person come into a real relationship with Jesus Christ and discover purpose and meaning in their life

What this means for you

As a leader, the biopsychosocial approach will serve you well as a model for understanding addiction and the core needs of the people in your congregation who wrestle with addictive behavior. The church is the ideal setting for a recovery ministry because there is already a community of loving, caring individuals in place. The values of physical, emotional, social and spiritual health are intrinsic to a community of believers who take God's word seriously. The recovery ministry is simply an extension of those embedded values, with a deliberate outreach to those bound by their compulsive behaviors.

I'll explain much more about this in future chapters. But, the centerpiece of building a church-based recovery outreach starts with at least one staff person who will act as the point person for establishing and promoting the recovery ministry in the church. That is the focus of the next chapter.

Works Cited

Frontiers in Psychiatry. (2013; 4:36). Is "Loss of Control" Always a Consequence of Addiction? Retrieved Published online 2013 May 15. doi: 10.3389/fpsyt.2013.00036, from US National Library of Medicine: www.ncbi.nlm.nih.gov/pmc/articles/PMC3654310/

NIDA. (2013). What is Drug Addiction. Retrieved from Drugs, Brains, and Behavior: The Science of Addiction: www.drugabuse.gov/publications/drugs-brains-behavior-science-addiction/drug-abuse-addiction

Chapter 3: The role and responsibilities of the recovery director

Charlie attends a growing church of about 2,000 people in a large metropolitan area. It has been his place of worship for eleven years and he's happily served in various ministries during that time. To meet the needs of an ever-expanding congregation, the church staff has blossomed to 15 full-time pastors who are now trained and hired based upon their expertise in a given area of ministry. Each pastor has a designated life stage group that he or she is responsible for. The current ministries include: youth work, single adults, young marrieds, families, middle-age adults and older adults. They also have ministries that serve those grieving the loss of a loved one, those homebound because of illness and those recovering from divorce. Charlie feels fortunate to have a home church that makes a concerted effort to meet the many needs of the congregation and local community.

But, despite the depth of ministry outreach of his church, Charlie can't find an in-house ministry that helps him with a family-related problem. His twin brother, who also attends his church, is a closeted drug addict who keeps a low profile. He has attended this church for years but does not personally know any of the pastors. Charlie recently approached the pastor of family life and asked for some guidance on how he could help his brother. During their brief conversation, the pastor got out the local phone book and wrote down the numbers of three treatment centers in the area that he had "heard good things about from other people" and suggested his brother "check these out." When Charlie asked whether the church had any in-house resources they could offer, the pastor said, "We outsource these types of issues because we don't have the staff and expertise to help people manage their addictions."

Discipleship includes recovery
This story describes an all-too-common scenario across America:

churches striving to meet the many needs of their congregants but failing to see addiction recovery as a critical part of their overall ministry. I'm not suggesting that the church become a full-fledged addiction treatment center. The main job of the church is to expose people to the Gospel and create disciples. But, I believe that an important part of that discipleship process is being ignored when we completely "outsource" the care and support of individuals and families struggling through addiction. By inviting those with addictions to come for direction, support and encouragement we take advantage of an enormous opportunity to not only help them become free of their addiction but to show the love of Christ in a time when they are most vulnerable.

It is true that most church leadership teams are not adequately prepared to help people in their congregation who struggle with addictive behavior. It is not from lack of compassion or desire to see people change their lives for the better, but rather a lack of putting the right structure in place to address the specific needs of the addicted. This structure optimally involves having a designated staff member that becomes the public "face" of the recovery ministry in the church. This staff person could be full-time or part-time but needs to have a well-developed system in place that can address a wide variety of individual and family needs. This system anticipates the many points of contact through the recovery process: from the initial screening to long-term aftercare and all the steps between. Once a structure like this is in place, you are likely to see a steady stream of people from your congregation seeking help for their addictions.

I've talked to hundreds of pastors and church leaders over the years about the need for a recovery ministry in the church and I get the whole spectrum of responses: some instantly get it and think it is a great idea, while others express skepticism about its ability to work in a church setting. And because this is a new way of thinking about ministry, I don't blame you if you are on the side of skepticism. It undoubtedly is a stretch for many who do conventional ministry. But, if you'll stay with me I'll lay out the whole blueprint piece-by-piece for how it can be done and done well. Let me start by sharing a few facts that may help you to see why a church-based recovery ministry is not only a good idea but also a critical need.

The state of addiction in society and our churches
Let's begin by framing the addiction problem we have in society. According to the Substance Abuse and Mental Health Services Administration's (SAMHSA) 2013 National Survey on Drug Use and Health, 22.7 million people in the U.S. aged 12 or older needed treatment for an illicit drug or alcohol use problem. But, only 2.5 million persons actually received treatment at a specialty facility for an illicit drug or alcohol problem. That means 20.2 million people needed treatment for an illicit drug or alcohol use problem but did not receive treatment at a specialty facility in the past year (Substance Abuse and Mental Health Services Administration, 2014). What is most striking from this data is that only 10% of those who acknowledged a need for help actually got it. The other 90% either did nothing or very little to directly address their addictive behaviors.

So, think with me for a minute about those 20.2 million people who know they have a problem but don't reach out for help. What keeps them from taking the next step? There are many possible reasons but I believe the biggest obstacle is fear. They fear:

- possible rejection, ridicule and shame from others if they admit they have a problem

- the stigma that may follow them if they go into treatment

- feeling their real emotions that they typically numb with substances

- not having adequate coping skills to face life problems head-on without substance use

- the financial and work consequences of going into treatment

- the debilitating feeling of failure if they try to break the cycle of addiction but repeatedly relapse

The question I then ask is: What can churches do to help those people in our congregation (and there are a lot more than we realize) who are among those 20.2 million people who know they have a problem but are afraid to reach out for help? And, those 20.2 million people only include those with illicit drug or substance use issues. It doesn't even touch the millions of other people in our society who struggle with prescription drug addiction, compulsive engagement in sex, pornography, gambling, gaming or shopping. We as a society are saturated with addictive behavior to the point that it is often hard to recognize it. And we can't afford to be naïve to think that people in our congregations are not a reasonable cross-section of the larger society.

So, how well are churches doing in addressing this crushing burden of addictions in the larger culture and in their congregations? Not very well. One of the main issues is that church leaders don't seem to have a pulse on how prevalent addiction-related behavior is in their congregation. One glaring example would be the use of pornography among congregants. A 2011 survey by Lifeway Research in Nashville asked 1,000 pastors whether they believe that use of pornography has adversely affected the lives of their church members. Not surprisingly, 69% of those surveyed agreed. Yet, when those same pastors were asked to estimate the percentage of men and women in their congregation who currently view pornography on a weekly basis, 43% were unable or unwilling to respond (Lifeway Research, 2011). I find this troubling and also instructive. It tells me that many church leaders are not in touch with the addictive tendencies of the people they serve, counsel and shepherd.

On a broader scale, we could ask how churches are dealing with mental illness in general. Substance use disorders are a diagnosed condition found in the Diagnostic and Statistical Manual of Mental Disorders, 5th edition, which is the definitive reference for mental health professionals in this country published by the American Psychiatric Association. A more recent (2014) survey found that 66% of Protestant pastors rarely or never speak publicly to their congregation about mental illness. Yet, many people struggling with a host of personal problems seek counsel from their pastoral staff as a first resource. The study found that pastors desire to help those with mental health issues but only one-quarter of those surveyed had a plan for how to help individuals and their families. Only 14% had a counselor on staff that was skilled in how to recognize and assess mental health issues (Lifeway Research, 2014).

These statistics give important insight into the disconnection that I'm trying to highlight as it relates to addictions. People generally feel safe going to their pastor for help. That's the good news. But, only one-quarter of our churches have a clear plan for how they can directly help them with their mental health issues. What's more troubling is that only one in seven churches have a trained person on their staff that can even assess the mental health issue and provide an educated referral. This helps explain why churches are reluctant to get involved in a recovery ministry: they simply aren't prepared.

Think about the number of people who might call their pastoral staff for help with their addictions but never call an addiction treatment center. What if more churches had a well-developed system in place with trained staff to address the needs of those struggling with addictions? How many more people might break free from their addictions if the church offered services to help them and in a context with the support and love of a faith-based community? These are the questions that keep me up at night. This is the vision that propels me in my work and the core reason for this book.

In this chapter I want to lay in place the cornerstone for how your church can begin creating a structure to make addiction recovery part of the discipleship process. It starts with identifying the right person to be that public face of the recovery ministry and creating a place where people feel safe enough to come out of the shadows and admit that they need help.

Why you need an addiction recovery director

When I was the director of recovery for Henderson Hills Baptist Church in Edmond, Oklahoma, I became the face of the recovery ministry at our church. I was the designated point person for all things related to addiction. And, to get the word out, we openly invited people from the pulpit, in our literature and in our daily staff interaction with congregants to come and talk about any addiction-related issues. As I mentioned earlier, we got off to a slow start because people didn't know if they could trust the "help" that we were offering. But, within a short period of time I became overwhelmed by the number of people who came forward. Many of these people had been holding secrets about their compulsive use of alcohol, illicit drug use, prescription pain addiction, porn usage and gambling habits for years. Over and over again I heard the responses from people who were so thankful to have someone in the church to talk with about these issues.

I think specifically of Lauren who was a long-time member of the church. I had known her casually over the years but never had an in-depth conversation with her. I knew she was an intelligent, hardworking person and held a well-paying managerial job where she oversaw the work of 30 employees. She had also served on several committees within the church and was generally respected by all. What I didn't know, until our conversation that day in my office, is that she was addicted to OxyContin, a powerful prescription medication that is used to relieve moderate to severe pain. Three years prior she had been in a serious car accident that left her temporarily paralyzed for a few months. As she gradually regained her mobility and sensation, the pain in her back became unbearable. Her physician prescribed OxyContin to help her cope. Months of using the drug turned into years and though she was now mostly pain-free, she had become addicted to the drug and couldn't function without it. She was telling me a secret only her husband knew. She was pleading for help. I walked her through the steps it would take to break the addiction, found the treatment center that best fit her needs and supported her and her family through the whole process. She eventually stopped abusing prescription medication and got her life back on track. But, had there not been a dedicated recovery staff person in her church, the place where she had implicit trust and safety, I doubt she would ever have come forward to address her addiction.

Having a dedicated recovery director in your church sends a clear and powerful message to the congregation that addiction recovery is a priority within the scope of your ministry and that those who seek help will be treated with compassion and not condemnation (2 Corinthians 1:3-4). Having a recovery director also offers the church a tremendous outreach opportunity to draw non-attenders into the faith community where relationships can be formed by serving those with addictions and directing them to resources inside and outside the church that might help them.

Full-time versus part-time recovery director
For larger congregations of several hundred or more, a full-time dedicated recovery director is optimal. This full-time status affords the recovery director the ability to devote all of his or her time and energy to the task of meeting and screening new contacts, matching them with appropriate treatment resources, supporting them and any family members through the process of treatment, teaching classes on addiction recovery and training volunteers who wish to be part of this ministry. Taken as a whole, these tasks comprise what I have previously referred to as the full continuum of care. To be effective, we need to provide addiction recovery support and resources at each of these checkpoints. I'll delve into these specific checkpoints more in upcoming chapters.

For some, a full-time recovery director might sound like a luxury that a church can't seriously consider until several other key staff positions have been filled. And, I would agree. I'm not suggesting that you choose between a youth pastor and an addiction recovery pastor, for instance. I am simply trying to heighten your awareness of the importance of a recovery ministry in the church and encourage you to consider adding a staff person at some point who will take full ownership of this continuum of care so that the needs of people struggling with addiction do not fall through the cracks. If addiction recovery is not on your ministry radar screen, the resources needed to address those problems in your congregants will probably not be developed.

Though you may see the benefits of a full-time dedicated recovery director, your church may not be in a position financially or have the support of the elders or board to hire this person. So, what many churches do is start with a part-time recovery director to test the waters and see how the congregation responds. This person could be hired part-time or split their time between the recovery ministry and other staff duties. Though I try to encourage churches to start with a full-time director, a part-time position is movement in the right direction but can be very challenging. Virtually every church I know that has started with a part-time addiction recovery ministry and consistently applied the principles discussed in this book has realized their need to expand to meet the growing demand. That's good news. But expansion plans should be part of the long-term planning process even if you start small.

The last option for a recovery director might be to share a person between several churches. This person could be financially supported in equal parts by the participating churches to lessen the burden on any one church. A related option might be to contract with a trained mental health professional in the community that is experienced in working with addictions. This person might spend a day or two per month at each church performing screenings, doing basic counseling and making appropriate referrals as a way to serve local churches. Though you wouldn't think most professional counselors would volunteer that much unpaid time, you might be surprised. We'll talk more about this option in chapter 4 when we discuss the recovery director's networking responsibilities.

Necessary credentials for the recovery director
I will be the first to admit that the credentials of the recovery director are unique. You don't want just any person in this position; it needs to be someone who has a passion for helping people wrestling with addictions. In order to find the right person to head your recovery ministry, you need to be looking for specific qualifications. This person ideally needs to know how to fluently speak three "languages," as I like to call them.

Recovery minded
The first language is recovery. Ideally, the director's knowledge of the recovery process needs to be both academic and experiential. On the academic front they need to be well-acquainted with what recovery entails including, but not limited to, 12-step groups, such as Alcoholics Anonymous (AA), Narcotics Anonymous (NA) and Celebrate Recovery® (CR), to name just a few. Most people are under the impression that "recovery" is simply attending a 12-step group once you admit that you have an addiction problem. I wholeheartedly embrace the 12-step philosophy as part of the recovery process. It could be incorporated into the treatment process at any point but should most definitely be part of aftercare once treatment is finished. It is often inadequate when used as the sole means of treatment. This is a big misunderstanding that exists in the church: that addiction recovery is simply getting involved in a 12-step program. You need a recovery director who has an appreciation for the entire continuum of care, which includes aftercare, but is willing and ready to be part of each stage of the continuum.

Your ideal candidate should also have some experiential knowledge of recovery. Has he or she ever worked professionally or in a volunteer capacity with those in recovery? Better yet: has this person gone through their own addiction recovery process in the past? Prior addiction recovery experience is not mandatory. But those who have walked their own road of recovery often have the greatest passion, patience and compassion for those struggling with addictive behavior.

Mental health awareness
The second necessary language a recovery director should speak involves a deep understanding of mental health. Ideally, this person would have a clinical credential such as a master's degree in counseling or social work. At the very least they should have some clinical coursework or be a certified addictions counselor. This advanced training is important because the person in this role needs to know how to accurately assess not only the addiction-related behavior but other mental health issues that might co-occur with addictions. These could include depression, anxiety, eating disorders, or conditions such as schizophrenia, to name just a few. Our goal in doing screenings is to identify the person's core needs and find the best resources inside and outside the church to meet those needs.

In some cases it might be difficult to find a person with clinical credentials or a certification in addictions counseling to fill the role of recovery director. The church could then invest in the training of the best candidate by sending them to workshops, taking online courses or working toward an addictions counselor certification. The idea is that you want a competent person who is adequately trained to assess and plan a treatment path for each individual and family they attempt to help.

This clinical knowledge must also extend to an understanding of family dynamics. The consequences of any addictive behavior (especially substance use issues) have a significant impact on all members of a family. Whenever I have worked with an addicted individual that has a family, I don't have to look very far into their story to see the devastating effects of that addictive behavior on the person's marriage, their relationship with their children, or if it is an adolescent how it affects parents or siblings. Even worse, it sets in place a horrible model of how to cope with life for the other members in the family. The recovery director needs to be able to address both the individual who is addicted and the family system that is trying to survive in such a confused and chaotic environment. Addiction affects the whole family system. Unless the system gets healthier, the addicted person is at greater risk of relapse after treatment. We'll discuss the family system in greater detail in chapter 6.

This person's deep understanding of mental health also needs to extend to their own interpersonal skills and their ability to effectively relate to people in a personal way. This person needs to be compassionate, empathic, patient and able to speak the truth in love. Denial and distortion are constant companions for many people wrestling with addictive behavior and the recovery director needs to know how to confront that denial and clarify the distortions in a gentle and appropriate but truthful manner.

The recovery director also needs to have adequately worked through their own life experiences. This includes any patterns of family dysfunction, trauma or past addictive behavior. For example, people who grew up in homes where there was any type of abuse may be unclear about how relational boundaries best work. It is imperative that the recovery director understand relational boundaries to resist the strong tendency to try and "save" or "fix" the people they will be working with. It takes an emotionally grounded person to voluntarily enter into other peoples' stories of confusion and chaos and not take on too much responsibility. In addiction terminology this tendency to overextend ourselves is called co-dependent behavior. As a people helper, the recovery director strives for a relational boundary line that objectively discerns which aspects of recovery he or she is responsible to help with and which aspects of recovery belong to the addict. It is not always clear but the recovery director needs to know how to sort out these challenges, find that boundary line and be vigilant to enforce it. I'll talk more about boundary issues in chapter 8.

These are all important characteristics under the heading of mental health that churches should be mindful of when interviewing, hiring or contracting with someone to fulfill the role of recovery director for their congregation.

Theologically sound

The third and final language the recovery director needs to speak is theological. The person in this position needs to give clear evidence of a personal and vital relationship with Jesus Christ and be committed to nurturing that relationship both individually and in a community of Christians. If this person is a full-time or part-time recovery director, he or she should also be a committed member of that congregation. You can't grow the recovery ministry unless the director is continually visible and available to those seeking help.

The recovery director also needs a sound understanding of the Bible that ideally involves some biblical training. A seminary degree is optimal but not always realistic. I started my position at Henderson Hills Baptist Church with a lot less clinical and biblical knowledge than I needed. In my daily encounters with people that were literally fighting for their lives, I quickly saw where I was deficient and took classes for over two years to fill in my knowledge gaps. The development of a solid biblical worldview acts as a framework for understanding life's problems, including addictions. God's Word is the source of wisdom for helping people with their life challenges and providing direction in ways that bring hope and healing (Hebrews 4:12; 2 Timothy 3:16-17).

Primary responsibilities of the recovery director

I began this chapter by saying that the starting point for building a recovery ministry in your church is to find a person who is passionate about helping people with addictions and making them the face of the ministry. Without this person, it will be almost impossible to create the structure necessary for a full continuum of care. But, passion alone is not enough. Your director of recovery also needs to competently speak the languages of recovery, mental health and be theologically sound in his or her worldview. This may sound as though I am asking a lot. I am. But, what I am proposing could transform how we do ministry in the local church and begin to make a significant contribution to the massive addiction problems we have in our society.

I've mentioned the continuum of care a few times thus far, so let me summarize what that continuum of care involves and tie it in to the primary responsibilities of the recovery director. The recovery director is responsible to:

- Screen individuals, couples and families that come to the church for help with addiction-related issues. This screening includes identifying any additional mental health issues that need to be addressed as part of the treatment and referral plan.

- Create a comprehensive network of local and national resources that address the full range of addictions and other mental health issues (the focus of chapter 4).

- Make pointed referrals to the appropriate resources based upon the detailed screening.

- Provide ongoing emotional support to the individual in treatment and family members (if applicable).

- Monitor treatment progress and help the individual in treatment develop a reentry plan back into daily life (family, church, work, personal routine).

- Organize and oversee the aftercare ministries in the church, which could include one or more 12-step programs.

- Teach the church a biblical perspective on addiction and

recovery and how a recovery ministry can bring healing and hope for many in need.

• Train volunteers who wish to be part of the recovery ministry.

In the next chapter we will focus on how to build a comprehensive network of local and national resources that the director of recovery can use. This is a key component of any successful recovery ministry and one that will involve lots of practical suggestions for how to get started.

Works Cited

Lifeway Research. (2011, November 10). Pastors Say Porn Impacts Their Churches, Many Unsure to What Degree. Retrieved from www.lifewayresearch.com/2011/11/10/pastors-say-porn-impacts-their-churches-many-unsure-to-what-degree/

Lifeway Research. (2014, September 22). Mental Illness Remains Taboo Topic for Many Pastors. Retrieved from www.lifewayresearch.com/2014/09/22/mental-illness-remains-taboo-topic-for-many-pastors/

Substance Abuse and Mental Health Services Administration. (2014). Results from the 2013: National Survey on Drug Use and Health:Summary of National Findings. Retrieved from http://www.samhsa.gov/data/sites/default/files/NSDUHresultsPDFWHTML2013/Web/NSDUHresults2013.pdf

Chapter 4: Creating a reliable referral network

Greg has been an associate pastor at his church for seven years and is the go-to person for counseling-related issues. He didn't have a formal counseling degree but took a few counseling elective courses during his seminary training and occasionally attends workshops on timely people-helping topics. He is well-respected for his insights by the pastoral staff and considered by many in the congregation to be a sensitive man with excellent interpersonal skills.

One morning while Greg was in his church office, a married couple knocked on his door seeking counseling for a number of problems. The wife started the conversation but barely got the first sentence out before she broke into a deep sob. Over the next hour she explained, through tears, that she was on the edge of divorce because of her husband's multiple affairs, drug problems and crushing financial debt as a result of his compulsive gambling habits. They and their four children are facing foreclosure of their home because they have not paid their mortgage in months. The husband said little during the conversation but affirmed that his wife's accusations were accurate. He wanted help. This couple asked Greg if he could counsel them both for their marriage problems and the husband's addictions.

Counsel or refer?

So, to make this more personal, put yourself in Pastor Greg's place and answer the following question: Would you counsel this couple for their marriage problems and the husband's addictions? I hope your answer to that question is both "yes" and "no." You could start by learning more about their story, asking pointed questions and showing compassion for their dilemma. Then you do a comprehensive screening of the problematic behaviors to get a solid context for what is going on. This screening will provide insight into the specific type of help they need (this will be the focus of chapter 5). Once you've done the screening, you could arrange a few counseling sessions to provide encouragement, perspective, help chart a path for their marriage and determine treatment goals for addressing the addictive behaviors.

But, I hope you would decline the request to see this couple as their sole counseling resource because the breadth and depth of their problems requires more expertise than you have, given your limited training in counseling. Here's what you know just based on the initial meeting with this couple:

- The husband has at least three suspected addictions: sex, drugs and gambling.

- Their marriage is extremely fragile and on the verge of collapse.

- Their financial situation is very unstable with the looming foreclosure of their home.

- There are four children exposed to all of this chaos and conflict.

This short list merely introduces you to the presenting problems. You will inevitably see other patterns and problematic behaviors when you do the in-depth screening. You can see how quickly an untrained pastor could become overwhelmed by the complexity and depth of these and other emerging problems. As I mentioned earlier, it should not be the main mission of the church to become a full-fledged addictions treatment center or even a full-service counseling center. The main mission of the church is to make disciples. One significant group of people that often gets overlooked or dismissed in the process of discipleship-making is those struggling with addictions. But getting a clear picture of these addictions can be challenging. These addictions can easily be masked by other problems, such as financial issues, marital struggles, parenting challenges, etc.

Since most churches do not have their own counseling center equipped with trained, licensed clinicians that can effectively manage these types of situations, it becomes necessary for church leaders to know some reliable external treatment resources in order to make appropriate referrals. When I say, "know" the treatment referrals, I am not saying know of them, such as their contact information or geographic location. I mean meet the people, visit the places and become familiar with the specific services and specialties they offer. Look closely at their credentials, reputation and treatment record. All of these things combined give you the ability to make an educated referral that's much more likely to result in effective treatment the first time around.

Now, if you are like most people who hear me suggest this type of active engagement with referral resources, your response might be, "I don't have time for that type of interaction with potential referrals. I am already stretched beyond my capacity as it is." I get it. Church ministry always has more needs than people and time to meet all of those needs. This is just one of the reasons I urge churches to consider a full-time dedicated recovery director to head the recovery ministry. My first weeks as director of recovery at Henderson Hills Baptist Church were spent meeting counselors, treatment facility personnel, addictions specialists, and others. It was an incredibly valuable time and the best way imaginable to get started in a recovery ministry. As I got to know these people and the specific services they provided, I found that I was able to not only make extremely targeted referrals based upon the specific needs of the people I screened, but it also opened the opportunity for ongoing relationships with these resource people. Think of this vetting process for your referral network as your gift to those in your congregation who need counseling help. Your screening of these resources is time well-spent.

Building a referral network
Building a solid referral network takes time but it can be one of the most valuable assets to a church staff team that decides to step into a recovery ministry. There are two primary motivations for building this referral network. First, I think of Paul's words that remind us to recognize our limitations: "For through the grace

given to me I say to every man among you not to think more highly of himself than he ought to think; but to think so as to have sound judgment, as God has allotted to each a measure of faith" (Romans 12:3). Paul goes on to explain that we in the church are one body with many members. We are not expected to know it all or do it all, but we are to exercise our gifts and allow others to do the same. We need to elicit the help of others both inside and outside the church to meet these needs. Building a referral network acknowledges that the church staff cannot be all things to all people.

Our second motivation for building a referral network is for the benefit of our congregants who are seeking healing from their addictions. We owe it to those who are lost, hurting, addicted, broken and alone to come alongside them and offer them resources that can help them put their lives back together again. Philippians 2:4 says it best: "Let each of you look not only to his own interests, but also to the interests of others." When you can say to a person who comes to you for help, "I personally know a counselor or a treatment facility that is perfect for you and your needs," it instills confidence and hope in that person that far exceeds what a phone number alone can do. With this personalized approach to referrals you become a catalyst for healing. This type of individualized support greatly increases the possibility of that person following through on the referral and making progress with treatment.

So, where do you start? The best place to begin is by asking people in your community that you respect for names of counselors and treatment facilities. Word-of-mouth is always preferable to randomly searching online or in a phone directory, unless you are willing to go outside of your local geographic area for treatment. And even then, there are strategic ways to find those centers. I'll talk more about that later in this chapter. For local resources you can ask other pastors in the area for their recommendation as well as other professionals (accountants, lawyers, dentists, physicians) who may interact with therapists in the course of their business practices. Once you have a few names, the real work begins with contacting them and doing your own screening. Here's what to ask and look for in screening individual therapists.

Finding competent therapists

Most communities will have at least a few competent mental health counselors and larger metropolitan areas have many to choose from. The challenge is finding the best ones and getting enough information about each counselor to feel confident referring others. You are not just looking for people with credentials. You want mature, well-trained, professional, accessible, responsive and spiritually sensitive (ideally a committed Christian) people of character. Unless a colleague introduces you, your first contact would most likely be by phone or email. Here's a sample of what you can say to introduce yourself and your intention:

Hi Joe, my name is Chuck Robinson and I am the new director of addiction recovery at Second Street Church. I am in the process of putting together a referral list of counselors in the area that we might use in the future and wanted to know if you might be interested in being on that referral list. If so, I'd like to arrange a time when we could meet to discuss your practice and see if an ongoing relationship might be a good fit for us both. You can reach me at....

It's optimal to have at least a dozen therapists on your referral list but even more would add greater depth. You want enough diversity in your referral list to meet the broad range of needs you will inevitably encounter in your role as recovery director. You want both men and women therapists with varying degrees of clinical experience, treatment orientations and specialties. You also want to consider the ethnic and cultural issues of your community and include clinicians who can speak their language and/or know their culture well. It's also helpful to have a few therapists who are willing to slide their regular fee for those with financial limitations.

Remember, you are screening therapists to compile a referral list of competent clinicians, which includes, but is not limited to, addiction counselors. As I mentioned earlier, addictive behavior is often the overt symptom of other issues, such as depression and anxiety, so you want to make sure that the therapists on your referral list can effectively treat people with many different conditions in addition to some specialized training in treating addictions. You will need to ask therapists about their specific addiction training so that you will know their specialties and feel comfortable referring to them.

You may need to contact quite a few therapists to find the ones that you implicitly trust and that meet your criteria. What are those criteria? Here are the categories and the questions I would suggest you delve into to find those therapists.

Credentials
I'll be the first one to admit that credentials don't always tell you a lot about a person. I entered my position as recovery director with no strong academic credentials but I was passionate about helping people with addictions and their families. I eventually earned credentials to go with my on-the-job training and I've helped a lot of people along the way. But, in retrospect, I wish that I had received training before taking my position as recovery director. It would have significantly reduced the learning curve. So, while academic credentials don't tell you a lot, they do establish some foundational credibility for the therapist's competency. You want someone with either a master's or doctoral degree in counseling or social work with some advanced training in treating addictions.

Clinical experience
The amount of clinical experience a therapist has is important. I would typically not include a therapist on my referral list that has less than five years of experience. That isn't a hard and fast rule, but generally speaking, you are looking for seasoned clinicians. It's fine for you to ask a clinician how many years they have been

practicing and the specific title of their degree. It's also appropriate for you to present a case study of sorts to the clinician and ask them how they might handle the situation. I would choose a case study that matches their stated areas of specialty. For example, say the therapist works a lot with adolescents that have substance use issues. I might say, "How would you approach a situation where a teen's parents are ready to send him off to a military school because of his repeated drug use and disrespect toward his parents?" I would specifically be interested in how this therapist would try to intervene into this situation between the parents and teen. Does the clinician seem to understand some of the underlying issues behind the drug use and disrespect, like the breakdown of the parent-child relationship, drugs as a coping device, raging emotions as a sign of communication problems within the family, etc.? A seasoned therapist will feel comfortable entering into chaotic situations because they intuitively know how to manage conflictual relationships.

Licensing

When possible, you should strive to refer to a licensed therapist. There are many reasons for this but the two most important are accountability and insurance. First, a licensed therapist is regulated in the state where they practice. This means that they are accountable to the state regulatory commission for their license. To obtain a license they have to meet strict requirements in their training (by having an appropriate degree), supervision (most states require a certain number of hours of supervision before granting a license) and they must take a competency exam, which tests the clinician's knowledge base. This accountability to the state also requires them to adhere to a code of ethics. If they violate that code of ethics the state can revoke their license to practice.

The second reason to refer to a licensed therapist is for insurance purposes. Licensed clinicians can apply to insurance panels and, once accepted, can submit claims for their clients and accept reimbursements for services rendered. With the advent of the Affordable Care Act, mental and behavioral health treatment are included as part of the essential benefits required in new insurance policies sold on the federal health exchange as well as to patients on Medicaid. That sounds promising but it is not a guarantee that many disorders, including depression, bipolar disorder, childhood behavioral disorders and addiction, among others, will be covered. It's always best to have people contact their insurers before making the first appointment to be clear on their benefits, deductible and co-pay. But, the inclusion of mental and behavioral health in new policies increases the possibility that many of your congregants with insurance coverage could use their health benefits to offset the costs of counseling. Another option is to look for a church in your local area that may have a counseling center that offers a sliding scale for counseling based upon a person's ability to pay.

Here's a partial list of licensed professionals and the degree required for that title. The actual title may vary slightly from state to state.

- Licensed Specialist Clinical Social Worker (LSCSW) or Licensed Clinical Social Worker (LCSW) – Masters in Social Work required, plus supervised experience and continuing education

- Licensed Marriage and Family Therapist (LMFT) – Masters in Psychology and/or Marriage and Family Therapy required, plus supervised experience

- Licensed Mental Health Counselor (LMHC; LPC; LCPC or LCMHC) – Masters in Counseling and/or Psychology, plus supervised experience

- Licensed Alcohol and Drug Counselor (LADC) – Masters in Substance Abuse Studies with mental health emphasis, plus supervised experience

- Licensed Creative Arts Therapist (LCAT) – Masters in Art

Therapy, Music Therapy, Dance/Movement Therapy, or Drama Therapy, plus supervised experience

• Licensed Psychologist – (PsyD; PhD) – Doctorate in Psychology

Addictions training

Currently, the credentialing of substance use counselors varies quite a bit from state to state. The education requirements and the number of hours of supervised work experience and direct client contact are state-specific. This in turn determines the scope and limits of the substance counselor's range of clinical activities. There have been attempts by the Substance Abuse and Mental Health Services Administration (SAMHSA) to create greater consistency in the credentialing process by the various entities that license substance use disorder (SUD) professionals across the country. Though there is no national consensus that all states agree upon for credentialing, SAMHSA has created five levels of competency based upon education and experience requirements that may help you screen therapists with stated substance use specialty training. Here are the five levels:

• Substance Abuse Technician is an entry level position. It requires no clinical experience, and has a highly restricted set of clinical activities the individual can perform, mainly under supervision.

• Category 1: Associate Substance Use Disorder Counselor requires practitioners to have an associate's degree and includes a slightly expanded scope of practice beyond substance abuse technician.

• Category 2: Substance Use Disorder Counselors require at least a bachelor's degree; the individual has a broader scope of practice and is allowed to provide individual and group counseling.

• Category 3: Clinical Substance Use Disorder Counselors are typically not licensed but can perform the entire range of clinical functions, although only in a licensed program under the supervision of a clinical director. Requires a master's degree in counseling or a related field. May provide supervision to lower level staff.

- Category 4: Independent Clinical Substance Use Disorder Counselors can perform the entire range of functions. Must have a master's degree and are licensed and able to practice (and bill insurance) independently. The Independent Clinical Substance Use Disorder Counselor can practice under the auspice of a licensed facility, within a primary care setting, or as an independent private practitioner. (Substance Abuse and Mental Health Services Administration (SAMHSA), 2011).

There are additional certifications that qualified substance use counselors can obtain that enhance their credentials. In chapter 10, I provide a link to information on a variety of state, national and international bodies that offer licensing and credentialing for addiction services professionals.

Types of therapy
In your referral network you want to make sure that you have therapists who can cover the whole range of treatment options. These include:

- Individual therapy. Most therapists do some type of individual therapy, which involves working one-on-one with a client on personal issues. When interviewing therapists for your referral network it is important to ask if they specialize in a particular area (addictions, eating disorders, depression, anxiety, etc.) or specialize by developmental stage (children, adolescents, single women, older adults, etc.) and what type of training they've had in these specialty areas.

- Family therapy. Family therapy is typically a critical need when addictive behavior is part of a family system. At least a couple of good family therapists are an invaluable addition to your referral network. These therapists are also adept at handling family crises that erupt from addictive behavior, such as a substance relapse or domestic violence. You receive a bonus benefit if you can persuade a clinician who is a Licensed Marriage and Family Therapist (LMFT) to be part of your network.

- Group therapy. Group therapy can be extremely beneficial for individuals who have already gone through individual therapy or who are far enough along in their healing process to benefit from ongoing interaction with others. Many therapists facilitate groups on a variety of issues because they know how powerful they can be for the participants. Ask each therapist you speak with about groups they have led, currently lead or plan to lead. Some of these groups are time-limited; others are ongoing. Group therapy is also a more cost-effective form of treatment over individual therapy.

- Couples therapy (marriage counseling). Couples therapy may be an extension of family therapy or it may be distinctly focused on the couple's relationship. Again, most therapists work with couples even if they are not a Licensed Marriage and Family Therapist. I always ask therapists during my screening interview how they would handle a particularly difficult couple scenario to get a glimpse of their therapeutic approach. This scenario could include any number of problematic issues, such as a couple on the verge of divorce, the presence of domestic violence or one with a substance-abusing spouse.

No one therapist is likely to be trained in or offering all of these treatment options. In fact, it's preferable that you have a few generalists and a few specialists in your referral network. Just because you refer someone to a therapist, there is no guarantee that the referral will work. The therapist might not be taking new clients, have room in their schedule, be affordable, have the right insurance connections, or be the right personality fit for the client. So, this reinforces the need to have at least a dozen screened and competent therapists to call on that you feel are both clinically competent and ethically sound.

Christian faith

It may seem strange to some that I've waited this long to address the therapist's faith as part of the criteria for inclusion in the referral network, so let me explain. First, I believe that if you can find committed Christians who are also competent, adequately trained and have the appropriate credentials, by all means embrace them as your top referral sources. The problem that many pastors encounter, which I also faced as recovery director, is that this combination of a strong commitment to Christ with a solid biblical worldview and high competency in counseling skills and credentials is not an easy blend to find. So, when I screen therapists for a referral network I ask them to tell me about their relationship with God. If their response indicates that they have a vital, personal faith, I push in further with questions about the authority of scripture, how biblical principles might be applied to particular counseling-related issues, and how they might respond to people who don't have the same worldview.

If the therapist meets all of the competency criteria and is sensitive and receptive to spiritual issues, but falls short of being a strong believer, I will still sometimes include that person in my network. And here's the reason: If I had cancer and I had a choice between having a world-class non-believing surgeon operate on me or a moderately competent Christian surgeon, I would choose the world-class surgeon. I would ideally want every person I refer out from my church to be working with a committed Christian. But, if I can't fill my referral network with those people, I would feel most confident sending my congregants to a known competent, qualified therapist as long as I know that the client's faith is going to be respected and encouraged. In this type of situation, the spiritual integration of their treatment and recovery might be best handled by the recovery director.

Reputation in the community

This probably needs little explanation. But, I believe that a therapist's reputation in the community is important, especially if they have been in the local community for some time. No therapist is going to please every client just as every pastor is not going to please every congregant. But, you should ask a few people you trust whether they know the person you are considering for your referral network and whether they have a reputation for honesty, integrity and doing what's in the best interest of the client.

Insurance/fees

It's often helpful to know before you refer someone to a therapist whether that professional accepts insurance and, if so, which insurers they work with. This can be the difference between a smooth transition and unnecessarily delaying the treatment process. Whenever possible, I try to match the person's financial situation with what I know about the therapist's financial options. This means that you need to ask the therapist which insurers they work with, if any, what their fee-for-service rate is, whether they will slide the fee and do they ever offer pro bono counseling in special circumstances. Keep this information handy because you will need to refer to it often.

Gut feeling

Once you've gathered all of this information it may be very obvious as to whether you include or exclude a given therapist in your referral network. But, if you are on the fence, it pays to listen to your gut feeling. What I mean by this is to ask yourself how you felt in your interaction with this therapist. Would you feel comfortable opening up your life to them? Would you feel safe, attended to, validated? Could you see this person walking alongside you in your journey? Would they be able to support you as you face your fears and heal your wounds? If you are uncertain, then I would suggest you pay attention to that ambivalence and move on to other candidates.

Feedback and updating

I have one final suggestion about building your counselor referral network. Once you screen therapists and begin referring clients to them, seek out feedback from those you refer. Do they feel they relationally connect with the therapist? Are they making progress? Would you recommend that therapist to others? If not, why not? This information is valuable because the referral network is always in flux. People occasionally fall out of favor, move, get sick, retire, leave the network, etc. You must always be on the lookout for new people to add to your network. So, building your referral base is an ongoing activity. In addition, you should try to meet with your referral network in person at least once or twice a year to keep the relationship fresh and update any contact information, such as new treatment specialties, that might have changed since you last communicated. With proper consent and a signed release form you can also get updates from the counselor on how your referred person is progressing in their treatment sessions.

Finding treatment centers

More often than not, people with addictions, especially those struggling with substance use issues, are going to need more intensive help than what a counselor can provide in one hour of therapy a week. You will likely see how severe the addictive behavior is when you do the initial screening interview and this will help you determine whether an individual therapist or a treatment center is the most appropriate referral. But, it is inevitable that you will need a few solid treatment centers that you know and trust in your referral network.

You will apply the same hands-on approach toward finding appropriate treatment centers that you practiced with individual therapists for your referral network. The difference is that there are typically far fewer treatment centers in your immediate community than there are counseling agencies or privately practicing clinicians. And, as I will address shortly, you are not limited to only treatment centers in your local geographic area. It may be necessary to go a longer distance to get the best treatment for a particular person and condition. Regardless of whether the facility is local or farther away, here are some of the criteria you should use.

- Is the facility accredited and licensed? Make sure the treatment facility is both accredited and licensed. State licensing is not the same as accreditation since states vary widely in their licensing requirements.

- What credentials and licenses does the program's clinical staff hold? You want to know what the credentials and licenses are for professionals providing treatment in these facilities. This ensures that the facility meets nationally recognized standards for professional practice. Some of the credentials held by addiction professionals in treatment centers include LADC (licensed alcohol and drug counselor), LPC (licensed professional counselor), CAC (certified addictions counselor), CDAD (certified alcohol and other drug abuse counselor), CADS (certified alcohol and drug counselor), LDAC (licensed drug and alcohol counselor), or CCDP (certified co-occurring disorders counselor).

- Does the facility have some statistics on their treatment outcomes? Look for evidence-based treatment centers that have research and statistics on items such as percentage of people who complete treatment vs. leaving against medical advice, outcome studies and the percentage of fewer drinking/using days post-treatment.

- Is medical detoxification ("detox") offered as a part of residential treatment? It is not uncommon that substance use treatment begins with detoxification, to help stabilize the person before beginning any formal treatment program. Detoxification involves stopping the drugs and allowing the body to rid itself of those substances that have been chronically used. Check to see if the facility's policy is to have the patient undergo a medical evaluation of their physical health and receive detoxification treatment if necessary. Some facilities will send a person to a separate location for detox and then transition them back into treatment when detox is completed.

- What specific services does the facility provide? You ideally want a facility that has a wide range of services. These could include:

  - Residential treatment – Residential treatment involves living at the treatment facility while undergoing intensive treatment during the day. Residential treatment typically lasts from 30-90 days depending on the situation. But there may be times when a person's treatment extends beyond 90 days, so there is no magic number that is right for every situation.

  - Partial hospitalization – Partial hospitalization is for people who require ongoing medical monitoring but have a stable living situation. These treatment programs usually meet at the hospital or treatment facility 3-5 days a week for 4-6 hours per day.

  - Intensive outpatient program (IOP) – In an IOP the person usually attends the program at least 3 days a week for 2-4 hours a day or a minimum of 9 hours per week for about 6-8 weeks. The major focus is relapse prevention. These outpatient programs are often scheduled around work or school.

  - Counseling (Individual, Group, or Family) – These treatment options should be in addition to the other types of treatment for the addiction or used as a follow-up type of support. The individual and family counseling that takes place in the program should work to identify the root causes of the person's addiction and help repair strained relationships in the family. Group counseling can be very effective at building healthier coping skills.

  - Sober living – Some facilities offer a program called Sober Living, which normally follows residential treatment. A

Sober Living arrangement consists of living with other recovering addicts in a supportive, substance-free environment. Sober living facilities are useful if the person either has nowhere to go following residential treatment or needs a transitional environment before returning home because the home environment is not conducive for recovery or increases the risk of relapse.

It's also important to know whether the facility offers a holistic approach to treatment. In other words, in addition to the physical and psychological issues that are front and center, will the program also incorporate a spiritual dimension into treatment? If so, what are the specific components of that integration? Will they also get educated on wellness issues? This holistic model is most likely to occur when a facility uses a multidisciplinary team of skilled professionals to address these different areas. A multidisciplinary team consists of professionals who work together to plan and assist in the treatment process for each person. Each member of the team meets individually with the person in treatment and then meets as a team to discuss the findings and form a treatment plan that includes individualized goals and objectives. This team might include physicians, psychologists, nurses, counselors, addiction specialists and administrative personnel.

• Is there ongoing support after leaving treatment? After detox and the formal treatment program, the individual is going to need aftercare, which often consists of any type of intervention that follows the initial addiction treatment, such as 12-step groups, counseling, skill-building classes, follow-up/check-ins, alumni services, outings, etc. In most cases, aftercare is thought of as only being involved in a 12-step group, such as Celebrate Recovery (CR), Alcoholics Anonymous (AA), Narcotics Anonymous (NA), Sex Addicts Anonymous (SAA), etc.

These aftercare programs are critical for reducing the risk of relapse. As I've mentioned, the church that has a recovery ministry should have a vibrant aftercare program as well. But, immediately after treatment, it may be preferable to have the person begin in the aftercare program that the treatment center offers. The reason is continuity. The person in recovery may need the familiarity of treatment center staff to eventually transition to the aftercare program at the church. So, in your screening of treatment centers, be sure to find out if they have an aftercare program and how it works. If treatment takes place some distance from the person's home, the continuity of care in the transition back to their home base may be divided between the family, the referring therapist and/or the recovery director. If the recovery director keeps in touch with the person during treatment, a smooth transition to aftercare in the church should help preserve that continuity.

Treatment centers outside your geographic area
Sometimes it is preferable to refer a person to a treatment facility in their local community. But, that is not always possible or preferable. It might be that there are no treatment facilities nearby that meet the above criteria. Or, a person may have a specific condition, such as a sexual addiction, eating disorder or gambling addiction, that requires a level of expertise that can't be found locally. Or, the person may simply need to get away from the negative influences of a dysfunctional home or peers that don't support recovery. Sometimes there is also a geographical motive to be in calm, private and inspiring environment particularly conducive to healing, such as near water or in the mountains.

It's better to encourage people to get the best treatment available, even if that means going some distance, than settling for mediocre treatment that is more convenient. I want to see people get the best treatment possible the first time around, which will save time and further deterioration of their condition, decrease the risk of relapse and be a better long-term financial investment than getting the most convenient treatment. When a person gets quality treatment and then returns to the church where there is a community of supportive, caring individuals who will hold that person accountable to their recovery goals and encourage them to actively participate in an aftercare program, you have a powerful recovery model in place.

Screening process for treatment facilities

Whether the treatment facility is near or far, you must take a slightly different approach to screening facilities compared to individual therapists. First, I would visit the Web sites of the facilities in your area to see the range of services they provide and the information they provide regarding the criteria mentioned above. For those facilities that score high on the list of criteria, I would then ask trusted people in your congregation and others in the community about the reputation of those facilities. Based on that feedback, I would take the top contenders and contact those facilities to arrange an information-gathering session. You can do this information gathering any number of ways. One way you can do this is to use a free online inventory called the Addiction Treatment Inventory (ATI) created by the Treatment Research Institute. It is a thorough questionnaire that walks you through all of the major services provided at a treatment facility. It takes about 20-30 minutes to go through and can be done over the phone with the program director, coordinator or even a receptionist, if they have enough knowledge to answer the questions. In chapter 10, I have provided the link to this document that you can copy and use for your assessment.

After you have gathered all of the information, if the treatment facility is local and you want to include that facility in your referral network, I suggest you make an appointment with the admissions director or marketing representative to introduce yourself, see the facility and ask any additional questions you might have. Most facilities are eager to meet anyone in the community who might be inclined to refer individuals to their program. Think of this screening process as part of building an ongoing relationship. Both your relationships with treatment facilities and individual therapists will prove to be an invaluable asset for you as recovery director and instill a great deal of confidence in anyone you might refer to these individuals or programs.

If the facility I'm interested in is outside the local geographic are and one that I've heard good things about, I will contact the facility directly to see if I can visit the facility. They may invite me to a one-on-one visit where I come by myself, or they may suggest I attend one of their scheduled professional weekends, where professionals come to the facility during scheduled hours, similar to an open house. Either way, being onsite allows you to meet the admission personnel, counselors and administrators and get a true feel for what the client experience might be like. Many treatment facilities will pay for your travel expenses, so be sure to ask when you contact them.

In the next chapter, we will explore the screening process that the recovery director uses to assess addictive behavior. We'll also take a closer look at screening tools you can use and discuss ways to measure a person's motivation for making the kinds of change they want.

Works Cited
Substance Abuse and Mental Health Services Administration (SAMHSA). (2011, September). Scopes of Practice and Career Ladder for Substance Use Disorder Counseling. Retrieved from https://store.samhsa.gov/shin/content/PEP11-SCOPES/PEP11-SCOPES.pdf

Chapter 5: The screening/assessment process

Imagine that you're in your church office and a middle-age woman knocks on your door asking if you have a few minutes to talk. She tells you that she has an alcohol problem and that she needs some help to get her life back on track. She asks if there is any counseling at the church or an AA group she could get involved with. You ask a few questions about the extent of her drinking and her family life to get a larger context for the problem. Convinced that she needs help, you tell her that no one on the church staff has experience doing ongoing substance-related counseling but there is an AA meeting in the church that meets on Friday evenings. For counseling, you suggest a local hospital that has a substance use program and give her the number. As she leaves you hope she follows through on the referral and the AA group, but you probably will never know the outcome.

In most churches, the above conversation (which lasted about 15 minutes) would be as close to a formal screening as anyone might get, especially if it relates to substance use issues. Most pastors are quick to refer addiction-related behavior to sources outside the church largely because they don't know what to do with these types of problems.

But, there is an alternative. Let's replay the same scenario so I can show you how this conversation could be more supportive and result in a different outcome. It's possible to come alongside a person seeking help and keep them in the church instead of sending them away. This in turn greatly increases the likelihood of them getting the help they need.

Scenario rebooted
So, after this same woman tells you that she has an addiction to alcohol and you ask a few questions to get a larger context for her situation, you say the following: "Based on what you've told me, it does seem that alcohol is a problem, not only for you but also for your family. I'd like to help you. We do have some resources

here at the church that you could take advantage of, which include short-term counseling, a couple of 12-step programs and a great, supportive community of people who are compassionate toward those struggling with addictive behaviors. We also have an extensive referral network of therapists and treatment centers that we've personally screened for their expertise and competency. But, before I just start recommending things for you to get involved in, I'd like to make sure my suggestions are best suited for your specific needs. The best way to do that is to conduct a screening interview to better understand the extent of your alcohol problem and get clarity on any other issues that might be related. It would take about an hour to go through these questions and would give me a much clearer picture of how I might be able to help you. Would you be willing to walk through that process with me?"

If you compare the two conversations it's pretty easy to see a stark contrast between them. In the first example, the woman leaves your office after a brief 15-minute conversation with only a piece of paper that lists the phone number of the treatment center and the time of the weekly AA meeting. Her hopefulness about breaking the addictive tendencies in her life has not increased at all because the church doesn't offer her any real help or resources. So, she continues her search – alone.

In the second example, the same woman is encouraged to tell her story at greater length through the screening process. She no longer needs to feel alone because she has found a community of people who will come alongside her to support her through this process. She doesn't need to leave to continue her search elsewhere because the church offers multiple resources to help her find just the right recovery path for her situation. For the first time in many years she is hopeful that she can get her life, and possibly her faith, back on track.

This second example is what I envision for your church and many churches throughout the country. I would like your first point of contact with people to be one that instills hope that they can overcome their addictions. So many of those wrestling with addictions have repeatedly tried and failed to break free and they no longer believe they are capable of escaping the prison of their addiction.

In this chapter I want to show you why doing a screening interview is useful for helping to make educated referrals. I also want to expose you to some tools that you can use to make the screening process easy and consistent.

Why start with a screening interview?

A screening interview is your best way to understand the context of how certain life events and behaviors are related to a congregant's presenting problem of addiction. It's important to remember that a screening interview in your church office is not intended to formally diagnosis anyone's mental condition. I am assuming that you're a pastor or someone with limited understanding of clinical issues and not a licensed therapist. Therefore, you are not in a position to make a formal diagnosis. But you can make an educated referral to one of your vetted therapists or treatment centers based upon the information you gather. So, the point of the screening is not to be comprehensive but rather to gather enough information to help the person find the best path toward recovery for their needs. Too many referrals are quickly and haphazardly made without having a clear and accurate understanding of a person's current life context.

Confidentiality and informed consent

Even though you are not a licensed counselor, it is still important that you approach the screening process with professionalism. People will be sharing personal information about themselves in the screening interview and that information needs to be treated with great respect. The HIPAA Privacy Rule that prohibits the sharing of personal information directly applies to health plans, health care clearinghouses, and any health care provider who transmits health information in electronic form. Based on this definition, most congregations would not be subject to the requirements of the Rule. In my suggested set-up of a church-based recovery ministry, the local church is not attempting to be a clinic or a formal counseling ministry. There is a screening process but that is for the purpose of targeted referrals. Periodic counseling between the recovery director and someone seeking recovery assistance would not qualify as a "counseling center" and would not fall under HIPAA Rule. Some state laws may limit disclosures and it is advised that you check those laws in your state.

To add a level security, I recommend getting a signed informed consent form before doing a screening interview. This form should clearly spell out the purpose and limits of the screening and eliminate any disclosures issues moving forward. Below are some considerations for what you might include in that informed consent form. There is a link in chapter 10 to a document that further describes how HIPAA Rule applies to the church and a sample informed consent form that you can copy or modify for your own use.

1) Any documents or records you keep regarding the information you collect must be kept in a secure place, such as a locked filing cabinet or, if stored digitally, it should be encrypted with a secure password.

2) Before you do the screening, certain information (called an informed consent form) should be shared with the person. This document is intended to clearly state the parameters of what the screening entails, why you are doing it and what the respondent can expect as a result of going through this process. The informed consent document should include:

• What you will do with the information you gather. You should say that it is only for referral purposes and is not in any way designed to diagnose or directly treat any condition.

- The information gathered will be held in strict confidence and securely stored. The information will not be shared with anyone else in the church. The only exception might be a consultation with the screening staff person's supervisor or one of the church's referring therapists, if necessary, and only for the stated purpose of finding the best available referral for that person. The same strict confidentiality would extend to any person consulted.

- There are legal exceptions to this confidentiality, which include: 1) when the information relates to a clear and present danger of harm to oneself or others; 2) mandated reporting of threats of violence, harm, or abuse and neglect (from evidence or suspicion); and 3) other disclosures that may be required by law. You can say that such disclosures will be made to an appropriate authority and will be limited to material directly pertinent to the reduction of that danger. This section in the informed consent makes the person aware from the beginning that if they disclose their intention to hurt themselves or someone else, you will be required to report it to the appropriate parties.

- How long the screening process will last. Typically the screening interview takes about one hour but can be modified to what seems appropriate.

- Whether there is a fee for the screening. Most churches would provide this screening as a free service to help people in their congregation and community find the appropriate resources to begin healing from their addictions. If you wanted to charge a fee, you would want to make this clear in the informed consent form.

- What the respondent can expect after the screening process. The purpose of the screening is to point them toward the resources best suited for their recovery. You might want to say that upon conclusion of the screening they will be given the appropriate resources that might include one or more referrals to local therapists, 12-step programs, treatment centers, study materials or in-church resources that may be available.

• Obtain a signature from the respondent indicating that he or she understands the terms, limitations and privacy issues regarding the screening. A signature by the respondent is simply their agreement to the terms stated above.

Screening tools

There are many different screening tools available, ranging from general to condition-specific. Some are lengthy while others are very brief and to the point. I recommend that you have a standard screening tool such as the Multidimensional Addiction and Personality Profile (MAPP) that you use for consistency in your screening interview.

Then, if necessary, you can supplement your basic screening with additional screening tools. For example, if a person comes in saying that they have an alcohol problem, you could first do a basic screening with the MAPP inventory and, if you think it would be helpful, do an additional screening using a tool specifically designed for alcohol, such as The Michigan Alcohol Screening Test. The basic screening test might be all you need for one person while you may choose to go into more depth with someone else whose story seems more complex. Or, if the person says they also have suicidal thoughts, you could add The Suicidal Behaviors Questionnaire to your screening to assess seriousness of intent. All of these screening tools are available online for you to print and use free of charge. You can find the links to these tools, along with an extensive list of other resources, in Chapter 10.

Here is an annotated list of the individual screening tools I recommend:

Multidimensional Addictions and Personality Profile (MAPP)

The MAPP is a highly reliable test instrument that has been used with hundreds of thousands of adults and adolescents within various settings for over twenty years. It contains 98 questions total and 56 questions from four areas typically associated with substance use disorders. The test can be completed in less than thirty minutes, either individually or in a group setting. The design of the instrument allows the interviewer to identify nine patterns of deceptive answering and complete a visual item-analysis of every answer in less than two minutes. The MAPP comes with a referral guide that helps determine appropriate types and levels of care and is available in print or computerized format.

The Michigan Alcohol Screening Test

This is a 24-question self-report test that can be completed in 15 minutes or less. Each response has a designated number of points and includes a self-scoring legend at the end for tallying the results. This tool can give you a quick and reasonably accurate assessment of whether there is an alcohol problem.

The Suicidal Behaviors Questionnaire

This brief questionnaire has only four questions and is intended to be a self-report questionnaire. The respondent has several options for each of the questions and each option has a designated point total. The higher the final score, the greater the risk of suicidal action. The questionnaire also has an accompanying scoring sheet.

Conducting the screening

How you perform the screening is a matter of personal preference. There is no one "right" way to do it. All of the screening tools I've mentioned above are meant to be filled out by the respondent. Some screeners might select certain sections for the person to fill out while asking other questions verbally. I prefer to let the person fill out the form and then follow up with additional questions in areas that need more explanation or seem to contradict some other piece of information I've gathered.

A tool such as the Suicidal Behaviors Questionnaire is meant to be a supplement to the basic screening and only used when necessary.

Sharing the results of the screening

Once you've completed the amount of screening you believe is necessary, you will want to share your findings with the respondent. Remember, the purpose is not diagnostic but for referral purposes. So, you want to focus on summarizing the results in a brief statement and then make your treatment recommendations. Emphasize how your suggestions specifically relate to the items that came from the screening interview. For example, if the person has long-term alcohol and drug abuse issues, you might refer them to a reputable residential addiction treatment program that your church has an established relationship with. If this person also has marital and parenting issues, you might tweak that referral to a residential addiction treatment program that is known to have a good marriage and family therapy component to their inpatient treatment program. This referral process works most efficiently when the person screening and referring is the same person that develops the ongoing relationships with these referral sources.

Assessing a person's motivation for behavioral change

When doing a screening it can be difficult to really tell what level of motivation a person has for making the desired changes in their life. But motivation is a key factor in whether a person will take the necessary steps to realize the change they want. People with addictions are famous for good intentions but short on consistent follow-through. So, how can you accurately assess a person's level of motivation for change during and after the screening interview?

I have found one particular model, called the Stages of Change Model (SCM), very helpful. It was developed in the late 1970s and early 1980s by James Prochaska and Carlo DiClemente at the University of Rhode Island where they were studying cigarette addiction. Since then, SCM has been applied to a wide range of issues, including virtually all addictive behaviors, weight loss, self-harm and a host of other behavior-oriented choices.

The basic idea behind SCM is that behavior change does not happen simply because we have enough willpower or resolve. Behavior change is a process that must evolve through different stages. To better understand how it works and how you can use it to assess a person's motivation level for change, we need to understand how motivation follows a logical progression.

The stages of change
Here are the five stages of change in SCM. I'll list them here and then explain each one in detail with an example of how they might play out in the screening interview and into treatment.

- Stage 1: Precontemplation – At this stage a person does not acknowledge a problem, so no behavior change is expected.

- Stage 2: Contemplation – In this stage there is some acknowledgement of a problem but the person is thinking or contemplating whether it is serious enough to warrant behavioral change.

- Stage 3: Preparation – In this stage there is clear acknowledgement of a problem and the person makes small changes while preparing to make more significant changes.

- Stage 4: Action – In the action stage, the person shows full ownership of the problem by doing whatever is necessary to address the problem(s).

- Stage 5: Maintenance – The maintenance stage is where the progress made in the action stage is maintained while the person attempts to increase their insight into related issues.

A quick glance at these stages could lead you to the conclusion that it's the action stage where real behavior change takes place. While there is a kernel of truth to that observation, this model takes a different approach. Those that use this model believe that all of the stages of change are critical because one builds on the next. It is the progression that matters most: from not seeing the problem to thinking about it and then making small changes that can eventually lead the person to measurable change. But you need all of the preceding stages (precontemplation, contemplation and preparation) in order to get to that radical shift in behavior that occurs in the action stage.

It would be ideal if every person who reached the contemplation stage (having some recognition of the problem) went on to the preparation and action stages to break free of their addictive behaviors. But, as we know, that doesn't happen very often. There is nothing magical or automatic about people reaching a particular stage that propels them to the next stage. People can get stuck in the contemplation and preparation stages for long periods of time. They can also revert back to previous stages. For example, say a young man reaches the preparation stage, which is indicated by his willingness to significantly cut back on his alcohol usage. Then he hits a patch of particularly stressful days at work and goes on a drinking binge. This puts him back in the contemplation stage. He knows he has a problem but isn't taking any responsibility at present for making a change. This back and forth toggling between stages is not uncommon depending on the type of addiction and the emotional stability of the person.

Take Adam, for example, who is addicted to crack cocaine and methamphetamine. When he first came to our church he acknowledged that he had a drug problem and wanted help. I mentally placed him in the contemplation stage at our first contact. He was at that time cutting back on meth and cocaine in an effort to eventually stop. I did the initial screening with him and suggested a terrific treatment center where he could go through detox and then inpatient treatment. He told me he needed time to think about it. Three weeks later when I contacted him he said he was still "thinking" about it. I continued to stay in contact with him over many months and even in our last contact he was not ready to move forward with treatment. Of course, during this entire time he had continued using drugs. People like Adam get stuck in the contemplation stage because they are not ready to give up what they consider to be the "benefits" of the addiction, such as numbing their emotional pain, helping them cope with stress or tolerating unhealthy relationships. Yet they know they need help and this creates an uncomfortable tension.

Let me walk you through each of the five stages in greater detail and show you how these stages might present in your screening interview. In all of the following stages I'll use the example of a male in his 30s who has an alcohol problem. Notice how he has no ownership of his problem in the precontemplation stage and progresses to full ownership in the action stage.

Stage One: Precontemplation
In the precontemplation stage, a person is not thinking about change because they are not yet able to admit that there is a problem. A person at this stage tends to defend their behavior and may project blame onto others as if they are the source of the problem.

Example
Jim, a married man with three children, comes to the church to discuss a "problem" that involves drinking. You set up a screening interview and here's a part of the conversation that follows:

Pastor: You said on the phone that you have a drinking problem you wanted to discuss?

Jim: Well, actually it is my wife who thinks it's a problem. She thinks I'm an alcoholic because I like to have a few drinks at social gatherings. My wife is threatening divorce if I don't talk to someone about this. I don't want a divorce, so here I am.

Pastor: So, your wife sees this as a problem but you don't?

Jim: That's right.

This would be a classic example of someone in the precontemplation stage. Jim goes to talk with the pastor not to discuss his struggle with alcohol but to appease his wife. So, because no problem is acknowledged, there will likely be no change. He has no ownership for his problematic use of alcohol. The real problem, according to Jim, is his wife's overreaction to his drinking and her threats of divorce.

Stage Two: Contemplation

In the contemplation stage, the person is at least partially aware that there is a problem and there are consequences associated with their behavior. Because they are aware that something is not right, they spend at least some time thinking (contemplating) about their problem. Although they are able to consider the possibility of changing, they tend to be ambivalent about it. A person in this stage is weighing the pros and cons of changing their behavior but often reluctant to give up what they consider to be positive attributes of the behavior, such as being able to party with friends. Here's how the start of the conversation might go in the screening interview:

Pastor: You said on the phone that you have a drinking problem you wanted to discuss?

Jim: Well, I have a tendency to drink too much at social gatherings. My wife is the one who brought this to my attention. I come from a family of drinkers and it wasn't apparent to me until I embarrassed her and the kids at a recent outing.

Pastor: So, how much of a problem is this for you?

Jim: It's not always an issue but there are a few times during the year when I tend to drink more than I should. I think I can handle it on my own but I told my wife that I would at least talk with someone about it.

You can see that Jim is taking a small amount of ownership for his behavior but not enough to make any real changes. He doesn't defend himself or blame his wife as in the precontemplation stage. He is contemplating the situation but not willing to take any action at the present time. As mentioned above, Jim could remain stuck in this stage indefinitely.

On the positive side, a person in the contemplation stage is more open to receiving information or feedback about their behavior and may be open to interventions, such as counseling, to further reflect on their feelings and thoughts concerning their behavior.

Stage Three: Preparation

In the preparation stage, a person typically has made at least a partial commitment to make a change. Their motivation for changing is reflected by statements such as: "I've got to do something about this" or "This is serious and I have to make some changes." This resolve usually leads to the person taking small steps toward changing the problematic behavior.

Pastor: You said on the phone that you have a drinking problem you wanted to discuss?

Jim: Yes, I think I have a tendency to drink too much and it is starting to affect my family life.

Pastor: What specifically do you see as the problem with your drinking?

Jim: I don't seem to have a problem with beer or wine. I can stop after a couple of drinks. But it's the hard liquor that I have a problem with. I will drink mixed drinks or straight bourbon at night to take the edge off of a stressful day and I sometimes get verbally abusive to my wife and kids. I don't want to do this anymore. I have to make some changes.

Pastor: What changes would you like to see?

Jim: I am going to get rid of the hard liquor in my house so I don't have access to it any longer.

Pastor: What about the beer and wine?

Jim: I don't see this as a problem. My wife and I enjoy a nice drink together a few nights a week with dinner.

Notice that Jim's degree of ownership at this stage has progressed from where it was in the contemplation stage. Here, he readily acknowledges that hard liquor is a problem and leads to behavior toward his wife and children he regrets. But, he also is straddling the line. By saying that beer and wine are not a problem for him he underestimates his vulnerability to alcohol and his propensity for misusing it to cope with stress.

On the positive side, a person in the preparation stage is actually generating some momentum for change by the small ways they are attempting to deal with their problems. Not only are they in a problem-solving mentality but they are typically more open to education and resources you might offer, such as reading materials, 12-step support groups and a recommendation of counseling to explore their behavior.

Stage Four: Action
This is the stage where people believe they have the ability to change their behavior and are actively motivated to do so. Most are willing to do whatever it takes to make the necessary changes. For example, a man with a history of alcohol abuse who reaches the action stage might get rid of all alcohol in his possession, begin counseling, attend AA meetings, even be open to an evidence-based and biblically sound treatment center as well as other options that might help build a strong bridge to recovery.

Pastor: You said on the phone that you have a drinking problem you wanted to discuss?

Jim: Yes, I think I'm an alcoholic. I can't control my drinking, though I've tried many, many times. I always end up back in the same place. I'm on the verge of losing my family because of my addiction to alcohol and I want to turn my life around.

Pastor: What specifically do you see as the problem with your drinking?

Jim: I drink almost every day and consume anywhere from 5 to 15 drinks throughout the day just to keep functioning.

Pastor: What are you prepared to do to get sober and stay sober?

Jim: I'm willing to do whatever it takes.

Pastor: Okay. Let's take a closer look at what's going on with your drinking and your life in general so I can get a clearer picture of your situation. Based on what we discuss, I can then suggest some excellent resources that can help you get started toward sobriety today.

Some people move into the action stage over a long period of time while others may be propelled into the action stage by a crisis, such as being issued a DUI or threatened with the loss of their job. But, when a person has this much ownership for their behavior and desires radical change, it's important to move quickly and get them connected to the best resources available while their motivation level is high.

Stage Five: Maintenance

The maintenance stage is where a person successfully avoids the temptations to return to the old behaviors. The goals of the maintenance stage are to sustain the progress that has been made and continue to gain insight into other areas of life that may need to be addressed. For example, as Jim goes through treatment and becomes sober, he might recognize that his relationships with his wife and children have been badly damaged by his substance abuse. So they pursue family counseling to address these issues.

A person in the maintenance stage should actively be acquiring new skills, such as learning to healthily manage stress, to better deal with life and avoid relapse. They should also learn to anticipate situations in which a relapse could occur, such as hanging out with old drinking buddies, and prepare alternatives in advance. Maintenance of the newly acquired skills is particularly important in the aftercare part of treatment since compulsive tendencies could be transferred to other behaviors such as food, sex, etc. I will discuss the role of maintenance in aftercare at length in chapter 6.

Matching the stage of change with treatment recommendations
Knowing these stages of change has two main benefits. First, it helps you to accurately assess the level of motivation a person has for the change they need. The degree of ownership they have for the problem and the amount of responsibility they are willing to take to make the necessary changes gives you a good indication of their motivation.

The second benefit of knowing the person's stage of change is it helps you craft your treatment recommendation. In other words, you want to match your suggested treatment modality to the actual stage the person is in. If you fail to consider the stage of change they are in, you can easily recommend a plan they are not ready for and end up being an obstacle instead of a catalyst in their healing. For example, recall Jim's level of ownership for his drinking problem when he was in the contemplation stage. He said that he did, on occasion, drink too much but felt he could handle it by himself. He's telling the pastor in a muted sort of way that he's not ready for any radical change. If the pastor had responded by saying, "Jim, I have to tell you that you are in denial and you need to get into an intensive treatment center for your alcoholism," I sincerely doubt that Jim would have even continued the conversation much less taken the pastor's advice. Why? Because Jim is in the contemplation stage and the pastor is working from the action stage. These are two parallel tracks that never have an intersecting point.

A better approach would be for the pastor to first consider Jim's current stage of change and then respond with suggestions that reflect the emotions and behavior of that stage. So, for someone in the contemplation stage, who is thinking about change but not ready to make any, the screening summary might include less action points and more affirmation. The pastor could affirm his honesty and his willingness to come in and talk. He could empathize with Jim's family issues and the regret he feels. He might suggest some reading materials or invite him to come back for a follow-up conversation. But, the pastor would not want to give him a counseling referral, suggest a treatment center or try to point him to a 12-step group because Jim is not at a point where he sees his need for those resources. So, the idea here is to match the resources with the stage of change and look for opportunities to help build a bridge to the next stage of change.

In chapter 6, we will begin to put all the pieces of the recovery ministry together as we explore the continuum of care that is possible within the local church.

Chapter 6: Facilitating recovery through the full continuum of care

In previous chapters I have made reference to the idea that the church should attempt to provide the "full continuum of care" to people seeking help with their addictions. In this chapter I'll put all of the pieces in place to show you how that continuum of care might look. I'll track it from your first contact with a person all the way through to ongoing aftercare.

Part of my work as recovery pastor has included helping with plans for treatment for individuals headed to rehab. Two questions I often hear are, "Why can't I/my loved one just go to the treatment center we found on the Internet?" and "Why such a huge difference in pricing among programs?" I realized the importance of explaining, in layman's terms, the various levels of care available when treating an addiction. Although there is a great deal of literature out there that explains the various levels of care, I discovered that addicts and their families didn't want or need to know the formal criteria laid out by the American Society of Addiction Medicine (ASAM), nor was it appropriate to even explain what ASAM is to people seeking solutions to a crisis. They just wanted to get their loved one help and didn't understand why the treatment center down the street wasn't always sufficient.

Since many people are familiar with how hospitals work, I start with the analogy of someone who has broken their leg. If I break my leg, my treatment typically would go something like this:

1) Emergency room

2) Intensive care, where the patient may see a specialist like an orthopedic doctor

3) Regular hospital room to continue recovering, allowing specialists to continue the work done in intensive care

4) Rehab or physical therapy for the leg

With addiction, a patient may follow a similar course of treatment, but with different names:

1) Detox – the first step to respond to the crisis – which must be followed by longer term treatment

2) A specialized higher level of care, similar to intensive care, often referred to as inpatient or residential treatment, where patients see specialists in psychiatry and other areas based on their individual needs

3) Extended care, where someone with an addiction continues building on the foundation established in intensive care treatment

4) Sober living and aftercare, where the patient receives ongoing support and structure but is beginning to get back to day-to-day life

To help break down this complex system into easy-to-understand terms, I came up with a baseball analogy using the positions on the field as steps of treatment. Note this analogy applies most directly to the person struggling with primary drug or alcohol addiction. The plan of treatment may vary for a person struggling with a different primary issue such as a process addiction or mental health disorder.

Typically, what the addict wants is to hit the ball, run straight to third base, then head home and call it a "score." Often, they think, "I don't need meetings or treatment, I can quit on my own," or "I might need detox, but I don't need treatment." In the rooms of AA, they call that the "easier, softer way." It can take quite a bit of explaining to help people understand the long-term, multi-step process involved in lasting recovery.

Visitor's Dugout: Detox
Detox is an incredibly important first step toward recovery. Addicts and their families have a number of options, including

treatment centers that offer onsite detox as well as freestanding detox facilities near their treatment center of choice. Note that detox is just one small part of the game. Treatment starts here, but the addicted person must run the entire field before they can truly "score."

1st Base: Residential Treatment / Intensive Care

First base is similar to intensive care in a hospital setting. In addiction treatment, intensive care, commonly known as inpatient or residential rehab, typically lasts around 30 days. These treatment centers are connected with specialists who have master's degrees or higher and are specially trained in trauma, sexual addiction, eating disorders, substance abuse, and other mental health issues. This is where the person struggling with addiction will examine themselves and find the root of the problem.

At this intense level of structure and support, treatment is usually priced higher (rule of thumb, $1,000 per day). From the time clients wake up until the time they go to bed, each day is filled with various therapies and recovery-related activities. Depending on the center, there may be a lot of experiential work, so the client, who is having difficulty thinking, can actually experience the new lessons and learn in a practical way how to deal with real-life situations without drugs and alcohol. At this level of care, the client will receive 1-2 hours a week of individual counseling and 2-4 hours a day of group counseling.

2nd Base: Extended Care

After the client has completed intensive care in a highly structured treatment center, they need to "step down" to a less intensive level of care. Again using the hospital analogy, this is where people move to the regular hospital room. In addiction treatment, we call this extended care. Extended care usually lasts 90-120 days. This type of care entails about an hour a week of individual counseling, along with 2-3 hours per day of group counseling. Some experiential therapy is done, but the focus is on preparation for the sober living phase of care.

It takes at least 120-180 days to overcome post-acute withdrawal syndrome (PAWS), where our body is detoxed but our emotions still tell us that our drug of choice or addiction(s) are the solution to our problems, despite the fact that they've caused untold pain and suffering. There is no real "cure" for this irrational thinking except time and continuing to work a recovery program, both of which help the brain and body begin to heal. Over time, the goal is to have the recovering individual begin to respond out of a "new normal" rather than the "old self." We know, and science has proven, that this takes time. I am a strong advocate of long-term treatment because with a chronic maladaptive behavior or addiction, there really is no short-term fix.

Short Stop: Sober Living
For the chemically addicted, sober living is an absolute must. This is where the individual begins to practice what they have learned in the intensive care and extended care phases of treatment. They seek employment, learn to budget their money and pay rent. They live with other people in recovery, hopefully gleaning lessons from the accountability and supervision of the house leadership. During this time, the recovering person will learn from their good choices and from the bad ones. Hopefully, sobriety will be maintained, but if not, the person has a safe place to lay their head at night and safe people with whom to share their struggles and concerns.

In our community, we have a number of sober living facilities owned by different ministries and individuals. I generally recommend that the client go to sober living at a place that encourages spiritual growth along with attendance at Celebrate Recovery and other 12-step meetings. Preferably, there will be weekly Bible study and Step study groups, while the client is encouraged to attend outside meetings and get a sponsor. A sponsor is a person of the same gender who walks the newly recovered person through the mine field of emotional ups and downs of recovery.

3rd Base: Aftercare
I encourage people to attend a recovery meeting of some sort at least once per day. If they have participated in the recovery plan mentioned above, they should be around 120-180 days sober. Our goal is to get the person to one year of sobriety prior to them moving out of their chosen sober living home. Aftercare would also include the individual working with a local aftercare group with a local clinician, preferably the referent/clinician/pastor who helped the client find the treatment center they attended and helped develop the recovery plan. While the client is going to feel a new sense of freedom, their new normal will include recovery, recovery peers and recovery meetings. Recovery is intended to be fun – fun in fellowship, and fun in all things that we do. Aftercare is extremely important because it prepares the person to become a productive member of society.

Home
Home plate is a "score." The recovering person has successfully reintegrated back into day-to-day life and is a contributing member of society. By this point, our hope is that the recovering person has stayed in treatment for 120-180 days and habituated in sober living for at least 180 days, so now they are at least one year sober. Statistics show that a person's chances of sustained recovery dramatically increase after a year of sobriety, and each year thereafter, exponentially, as long as they continue working a recovery program and stay in contact with their clinician, pastor, sponsor and other mentors.

With these analogies in mind, let's explore in more detail the different components of the full continuum of care:

- Initial contact
- Screening interview

- Referral to appropriate resources for treatment

- Monitor referral/treatment progress and family support

- Encourage aftercare

Initial contact

In chapter three I discussed the importance of having a designated point person, such as a director of recovery, to be the go-to person in your church for people seeking help with their addictions. Any staff member can be a first contact person, but it is optimal to pass on all addiction-related issues to the one staff member who is the public face of addiction recovery in the church.

I look at my initial contact with each person, whether that person comes from within the congregation or from the local community, as an opportunity to instill hope. I try to be mindful of the promise mentioned in Jeremiah 29:11 that says, "For I know the plans I have for you, declares the LORD, plans to prosper you and not to harm you, plans to give you hope and a future." That is what I want to convey to people when I first meet them: there is hope for the future despite their current pain and discouragement. So many people with addictions feel defeated and ashamed and doubt that they will ever be able to break free of their addiction. How you interact with that person in your initial contact can be the determining factor in whether they continue to seek help or dive deeper into their addiction.

I have many stories where my initial contact with a person led to their involvement in our recovery ministry and a complete turnaround of their life. But, it doesn't always work out that way. I remember a woman I'll call Delores who approached me one morning saying, "A friend told me you help people with addictions. I'm an addict and have been for years. I can't go on living this way. What can you do for me?"

I looked at this woman and immediately felt great compassion for her. She was in her mid-30s but neglect and the chronic use of drugs gave her the appearance of someone 20 years older. We talked for about 30 minutes. I didn't do a screening interview but instead addressed her most urgent need: the despair she felt about ever being free from her addiction. I wanted her to know that I cared about her and that the church cared about people like her who needed help. I briefly told her that we had many resources in the church and in the community that could help her. She just continued to stare at me with a vacant look. As she left, I gave her my phone number and asked for hers but she declined to give it. I encouraged her to call me. I never heard from her again. But, I tell this story to highlight the fact that we never know whether our initial contact with people will put them on the path to recovery or simply humanize them by our compassion, kindness and empathy. Most of the time our initial contact will lead toward recovery; sometimes it won't.

Delores' story reminds me of the parable Jesus told his disciples about a man who was walking from Jerusalem to Jericho when robbers attacked him and beat him to the edge of death. As he was lying there, a couple of prominent people passed by but offered no help. Then, a Samaritan, someone least likely to help because of class differences, felt compassion for the injured man. He treated his wounds, transported him on his animal and put him up in a nearby inn at his own expense (Luke 10:30-35). There are similarities in this parable with addiction. People feel beaten badly by their addictions, sometimes to the edge of death. Most people pass by them not wanting to get involved. But a recovery director is the Samaritan, a person who sees the deep injury and the hopelessness of the situation and responds with compassion.

I try to take the mindset of the Samaritan in my initial contact with people. When I first meet someone with an addiction, I don't know whether they will even talk with me, much less let me help them get into treatment. But, that first contact is important. My responsibility as recovery director is not to push anyone into recovery but to treat each person with dignity and respect and be a resource for healing. I don't know whether Delores was ever able to break free from her addiction. But I do know that if we meet the brokenness many addicts feel with compassion, it is often enough of a bridge to bring someone to the point where they are willing to accept help and do the necessary work to break the bonds of addiction.

When my initial contact with someone generates interest in learning what the church can do to help them, I typically schedule a screening interview to get a broader context for their addictive behaviors and other issues that might be related.

Screening interview
In chapter 5 I discussed at length the purpose, method and tools you can use for screening interviews, so I won't say much more about it here. But, to review, the purpose of the screening interview is to give you enough information to make an educated referral to the resources that would best match their stage of change and ownership of their problem. In the screening interview you want to learn more about their addictive behaviors and any other life issues that may be important to know about before you make an educated referral. You gather all of this information through your screening tool(s) and then ask any pertinent follow-up questions. Then you take all of the information, summarize it and determine the best resources to recommend.

Referral to appropriate resources/treatment
When I use the term "referral," I don't mean that everyone you do a screening with is going to be sent to some type of treatment. As I mentioned in chapter 5, the purpose of the screening interview is to match the person's level of motivation for change with appropriate resources that meet the person's needs at that level. For some, that will mean referral to a therapist or treatment center; for others it will be scheduling another conversation and/or recommending reading materials, a 12-step group or a ministry

at the church from which they might benefit.

Having said that, I want to dig down a little deeper into the treatment portion and help you understand what addiction treatment looks like. It may involve a referral to a therapist trained in addictions but might also require significant intervention in order to break the addictive cycle and literally save the person's life. While you as director of recovery will not be actively involved in delivering any of these intensive treatment options, it's important that you understand the progression of this treatment both for referral purposes and to fully appreciate the treatment process that many people with addictions go through.

Treatment progression toward recovery

Treatment can involve one or more stages in the addiction recovery process. Some refer to this as the "continuum of care." The continuum of care refers to a treatment system in which clients enter treatment at a level appropriate to their needs and then step up to more intense treatment or down to less intense treatment as needed. Addiction recovery should be tailored to the specific needs of the person in order to be most effective.

Most treatment starts with detoxification but if detox is not followed with a treatment plan, it cannot be considered actual treatment. Addicts who complete detox but do not go on to counseling, rehab or some other form of treatment, have a high likelihood of relapse. This is because detox rids the body of alcohol or other drugs, but does not teach addicts how to live drug-free or address the underlying issues that led to their substance abuse.

Including the detox process, there are six general levels of treatment that can be part of the overall continuum of care.

- Detoxification

- Intensive care treatment

- Extended care

- Intensive outpatient

- Partial hospitalization

- Sober living

- Aftercare

Detoxification

When a person decides they are ready to deal with their alcohol or drug addiction, the first step they often must take is to go through detoxification, or detox. Detoxification involves stopping the use of drugs and allowing the body to rid itself of those substances. The detox process typically lasts 3-7 days but can be longer in some cases and require medical supervision. The challenge of detoxification involves managing the withdrawal symptoms, which can be quite severe. The length of withdrawal depends on the type of drug(s) used. Physical symptoms (for example, pain, insomnia, diarrhea, cold flashes and vomiting) can last anywhere from a few hours to a few days while the emotional symptoms (depression, anxiety, cravings, etc.) can last for weeks.

In some cases, the detoxification process can be managed in an outpatient treatment center if the facility has appropriate medical supervision. Most of the time, an inpatient treatment center with medical monitoring is the best option. Depending on the level of drug abuse, medication may be used to help ease the person's withdrawal symptoms.

Intensive care treatment

Intensive care treatment is where individuals receive inpatient services at a residential facility staffed by addiction treatment and mental health personnel. The patient's direct addiction treatment may also include educational and social skills training. Treatment is provided in a structured environment that includes attention to mental health and addiction-related issues.

Under the umbrella of "intensive care" there are two broad levels of care. The most intensive is medically managed treatment where individuals are hospitalized because treatment of their medical needs is the primary focus. Although substance abuse treatment is provided, it is not the main focus of the hospitalization. The second level of care is inpatient, medically monitored treatment for people with significant medical, emotional or behavioral needs in addition to their addictive behavior. Intensive inpatient treatment typically lasts about 30 days, but could last longer, and is often covered by insurance.

Extended care

Extended care can follow intensive care treatment and is used to continue the treatment in a residential setting. It might be recommended if the person is struggling with depression, bipolar disorder, post-traumatic stress disorder (PTSD) or other mental health concerns that might complicate the addiction recovery process. An extended care program helps patients take a closer look at the specific emotional, social and mental obstacles that may be hindering their ability to break free from their addiction. It typically involves a combination of individual and group counseling. Extended care also helps people develop healthy tools to manage stress and transition to an independent, sober life.

It's important to note that not all extended care programs offer a full range of mental health treatment, so it's always recommended that you ask about the spectrum of services if mental health concerns, beyond substance use, are present. Extended care programs typically last between 90 and 120 days.

Intensive outpatient treatment

Intensive outpatient treatment programs offer an intermediate level of care. For some, this is the entry point for addiction recovery while others may first have been stabilized in an inpatient or extended care residential treatment program and now "step down" to intensive outpatient treatment services. Others may need to "step up" to intensive outpatient treatment because the outpatient or community care they were engaged in was not adequate to maintain abstinence or provide the relapse prevention skills needed.

Generally speaking, treatment in an intensive outpatient program is designed to enhance coping skills to better manage sobriety and primarily involves group counseling. Particular services vary by treatment program but often include substance use screening and monitoring, relapse prevention training, problem-solving skills and management of addiction triggers and cravings, among others. Treatment typically takes place at least 3 days a week for 2-4 hours a day or a minimum of 9 hours per week for about 6-8 weeks. The program allows participants to stay in their own homes at night and possibly schedule around work hours. This also enables the person to immediately incorporate their treatment principles in the real world of work and family.

Partial hospitalization
Partial hospitalization is designed for people who require ongoing medical monitoring but have a stable living situation. A partial hospitalization program will typically include individual and group therapy, physical and medication monitoring, education and aftercare planning. These treatment programs usually meet at the hospital or treatment facility 3-5 days a week for 4-6 hours per day and also allow the participant to stay in their own home at night. A person's participation in either intensive outpatient or partial hospitalization may be adequate to help them rebalance their life. But, if either of these approaches fails to provide sustained recovery, a "step up" to a residential treatment program may be necessary.

Sober living
A sober living facility acts as an interim environment for the person in recovery between extended care and a return to their former life. Some extended care programs have a sober living

program that is available following treatment but there are also sober living programs that are independent of these facilities. Whether part of extended care or a standalone program, sober living is intended to be a safe, supportive and structured place where people can live for a period of 3-6 months while they work on maintaining their sobriety and transitioning back into mainstream society.

Most sober living programs have standards that have to be met in order to stay there. These standards may be similar to those experienced in the extended care program. For example, most require residents to participate in a 12-step program, take frequent drug tests and demonstrate their commitment to ongoing sobriety by how they conduct themselves at the facility. Research has shown that recovering addicts who pass through some kind of structured halfway house environment, such as a sober living program, are significantly less likely to relapse, be arrested or end up homeless later on. The key protective factor is the positive community support that is found in many of these sober living environments (Polcin, 2010).

Aftercare

Aftercare typically refers to any type of outpatient intervention that follows the initial addiction treatment. Aftercare includes 12-step groups, such as Celebrate Recovery (CR), Alcoholics Anonymous (AA), Narcotics Anonymous (NA), and Sex Addicts Anonymous (SAA), but can also include counseling, skill-building classes, follow-ups/check-ins, alumni services, social outings, and other sobriety-enhancing activities and resources.

Many people assume that aftercare is the primary treatment for those recovering from addictions and all it requires is regular attendance at 12-step meetings. This misconception stems from a general lack of understanding about the recovery process and the critical role inpatient and outpatient treatment programs can play, when necessary, in the overall recovery process.

It is important that we think of aftercare as a vital part of recovery that usually happens after the initial treatment intervention. It is best utilized to help the person transition back to their normal life. But, for some people, the options typically associated with aftercare may be the only options a person has due to financial constraints or lack of insurance. In these situations, it is better to get involved in aftercare-related interventions than do nothing to address the addictive behavior.

Some people mistakenly believe that their recovery is completed when they reach aftercare. In reality, the real work of recovery is just starting. The biggest challenge in addiction recovery is learning to manage life's challenges with new skills, habits and relationships that support ongoing sobriety. Aftercare is where you can find ongoing help to do that.

Tracking the referral/treatment progress and family support
The next piece in the continuum of care model involves tracking the referred person's treatment progress while also keeping a pulse on how family members are doing. I believe this is a very important part of the ongoing care we can provide through the recovery ministry, but it must be approached with clarity and sensitivity.

Tracking treatment progress serves three primary purposes. First, it shows support for the person receiving treatment and their family. Second, it better prepares you to help that person assimilate back into the church and aftercare once treatment is completed. Third, it enables the church ministry to collect outcome data for the treatment modalities that are used to help church members.

So, the motive for keeping in touch during treatment is to be supportive and help with future transitions. But how you go about pursuing that contact during treatment usually determines whether it is perceived as supportive or intrusive. Some people long for contact during treatment and will take any opportunity to interact with you. Others will seem to disappear and go into hiding. Before a person enters treatment, I usually offer them the option to keep in touch but I always let them know that they will have to initiate the contact. I do this because I want the boundary line in our relationship to be clear from the start. I want to emotionally support them and their family members through treatment, but I don't want to foster unnecessary dependence or interfere with treatment in any way. Keeping these relational boundaries clear and clean is an important topic that I will discuss at greater length in chapters 7 and 8.

There may be instances where you need to talk with the provider of care (counselor, treatment program staff, etc.) or the provider may want to talk with you about something related to the person's treatment. This is possible if the person in treatment signs a release of information form that gives both parties permission to speak. The clinical provider of care usually has these on hand. This permission may be open-ended, meaning anything related to care could be discussed, or it may only pertain to certain aspects of treatment, such as test results or dates of service. It is recommended that there always be an end date and that you specify who the clinician can speak with.

If this need does arise, you should always have a copy of the signed release in your possession before you have the conversation. I remember one instance where a pastor was told by a counselor that he had "permission" to talk about one of his congregants. As it turned out, that counselor had only gotten verbal consent to talk with the pastor and when the counselee eventually found out that the counselor and pastor consulted on her case, she immediately felt that confidentiality had been broken. And she was correct. Verbal permission is not the same as written permission. Both parties should always have a signed copy of the release form before talking to each other.

Encourage aftercare

As I mentioned earlier in this chapter, aftercare is a vital part of treatment and critical for the prevention of relapse. One of the best ways you can encourage aftercare for people in your congregation is to have a thriving aftercare program in your church. For starters, form at least one 12-step program with people from the congregation who are already in recovery and can provide some organizational leadership to get it off the ground. Many churches have found Celebrate Recovery, which is a biblically based approach to aftercare recovery that applies scriptural support for a revised version of the 12-steps, to be very helpful. Celebrate Recovery has its own copyrighted materials that must be used if you adopt this program. You could also have other 12-step groups such as Alcoholics Anonymous (AA) or Narcotics Anonymous (NA) as part of your aftercare program.

You can also be creative with aftercare. As I mentioned in chapter 1, when I was the recovery director at Henderson Hills Baptist Church, not only did we have a thriving Celebrate Recovery ministry, we also had a Saturday evening adult Bible study class made up entirely of people in recovery. You can also make it educational with or without a Bible study. This was part of the way we supported addicts and their families in their journey toward healing.

In addition, we created two sober living homes that now have evolved into an apartment complex. Everyone who is part of that sober living facility is required to attend church, daily AA meetings and a weekly Celebrate Recovery meeting that included the Celebrate Recovery Step Study. Our aftercare program was committed to integrating sobriety with an overt Christian message of having a relationship with Jesus Christ and relying on the power of the Holy Spirit for strength, courage and discipline on the road to recovery. In chapter 10, you can find contact information for Celebrate Recovery and several other 12-step groups.

Avoiding relapse

A relapse can be defined as a return to substance use following a period of sustained abstinence. No person or family that lives through a perpetual cycle of addiction and then intensive treatment wants to consider the possibility of relapse. But we need to face the facts. Relapse is a very real possibility. The National Institute on Drug Abuse reports that 40-60% of people with addictions relapse back into substance use after rehabilitation (National Institute of Drug Abuse, 2008). Does that mean it will happen to about half the people you refer for treatment? It's possible, but not likely if you have a healthy and vibrant recovery ministry in your church. Here's why.

The highest risk of relapse is in the first 30-90 days following discharge from rehab. If you think about it, this period of increased risk makes sense. The person has spent weeks or possibly months working hard in treatment to get off substances and deal with deep emotional wounds. They've done this work in a very supportive environment with lots of accountability, encouragement and guidance. When treatment is over, the person reenters their familiar life that is often full of what we in the addiction field call "triggers." A trigger is a person, event or sensory experience (smells, music), thought or emotion that puts a person in touch with their old addictive behavior. It could be as simple as walking by a bar and smelling alcohol or driving through a section of town where the person used to meet up with drug-using friends. The trigger puts the craving cycle in motion. Once in touch with the old addictive behavior, the mind tends to lock onto those familiar ways and it becomes difficult to let go of these thoughts. The more the person thinks about them the stronger the urge to act out becomes. Here are a few of the most common triggers:

- Hanging out or socializing with old friends, family or others who currently use drugs or alcohol or have active addictions

- Visiting places where the person used substances in the past

- Exposure to high levels of stress

- Being in situations where sensory experiences, such as the smell of alcohol or cigarette smoke, heighten the craving for substances

- Experiencing difficult emotions such as anger, fear, anxiety, boredom or loneliness

The first 30-90 days following treatment is the time period when most, if not all, of these triggers might be experienced. This is why immediate involvement in sober living and aftercare are particularly important. If the person goes back to the familiar routine, people and sensory experiences without some help and accountability to respond differently to these triggers, relapse is very likely.

Post-acute withdrawal syndrome

The withdrawal process is another important consideration in understanding the risk of relapse. There are two stages of withdrawal that most people experience. The first stage is physical in nature and begins as soon as the person stops using substances. This withdrawal is characterized by physical cravings and may be quite intense. This stage may continue anywhere from a few days to several weeks depending on the type and severity of substance use.

Once the substances completely have been eliminated from the body, the second stage of withdrawal, called post-acute withdrawal, begins. The post-acute stage tends to be more emotional and psychological in nature, taking the addict through wildly fluctuating thoughts and emotions. This stage may be characterized by anxiety, sudden mood swings, poor motivation, fatigue, confusion, inability to concentrate, obsessive thinking and memory loss. These symptoms are typically more intense in the early months following treatment and gradually lessen over time. For some people, they may persist as long as two years. During the post-acute stage, the risk of relapse is increased.

The best way to prevent relapse during the post-acute stage is to help the person in recovery understand that these symptoms are to be expected so that they will not be surprised when they encounter the mental and emotional symptoms described. This will help normalize the experience so they can focus on managing the symptoms instead of reflexively turning back to substances to relieve their distress.

One of the best strategies for coping with fluctuating emotions and loss of concentration is to encourage the person to create balance in their life. They should avoid overscheduling their time to reduce the amount of stress they experience and focus on tasks that they know how to do relatively well. This will build confidence in their ability to remain in control of their life. In addition to familiar tasks, there should be ample time for rest, recreation and engagement in activities the person finds enriching, such as hobbies, walks in nature, social activities, etc.

It's also important to avoid substances such as caffeine and refined sugar. These substances can cause spikes in energy levels followed by crashes, which can make managing emotions even more challenging.

Finally, anyone in the post-acute withdrawal stage should be in regular contact with people who understand the mental and emotional challenges associated with recovery. These people might include an addictions therapist, a 12-step group, and supportive family and friends.

Here are some additional practices to help prevent relapse.

Respect triggers

Another common set-up for relapse is when the person becomes overly confident that they are no longer vulnerable to addiction triggers. This usually happens after the person has been abstinent for some time, but could occur within the first few months depending on the severity of post-acute withdrawal symptoms. For example, the person may tell themselves that they can have "a drink or two" to help manage their stress or that it's okay to socialize with old friends in bars because they're "stronger now." This rationalization usually leads to relapse, but can be avoided by always maintaining a healthy respect for the addictive behaviors. I tell people, "You're always just one decision away from breaking your sobriety. Therefore, every choice you make is an important one." Encourage the person to create a deliberate plan to avoid as many of the people and situations that might activate one or more of these triggers.

Build a strong support base

Help the person identify and embrace the relationships that are supportive to their recovery and suggest that they let go of the ones that promote addictive behavior. This idea of "letting go" is not easy when they have long-term relationships that they care about. But, as the saying goes, "Real friends will support a person's choices to become healthy; if they don't, they aren't real friends." This might require the person to reach out and build new friendships based upon healthy interests, such as joining a walking club, getting involved in a church sports team, becoming part of a Bible study or volunteering for a community project. I can't overemphasize the importance of building this strong support base and doing it soon after treatment ends. Part of this new support base can come from connections in aftercare and a 12-step program, but the more people who can come alongside the person in recovery, the lower the risk of relapse.

Encourage healthy habits

It's important that the person in recovery replace their old substance-using routine with habits that reinforce their new goals and intentions. For starters, they can create a daily schedule where they block out time for those parts of life that are priorities, such as work, family, healthy eating, exercise, sleep, recovery meetings, Bible study and possibly meditation. Encourage them to buy an inexpensive planner (or download a free recovery app or other tool) and plot out those activities on a daily basis. This can be in addition to doing a daily inventory to reflect on thoughts and actions. This daily self-reflection is an essential part of a 12-step program and is the core principle of steps 11 and 12. When these priorities are perceived fixtures in the person's schedule, with a clear idea of when and how they will attend to them, they are much more likely to see these goals realized and feel motivated by their efforts. This structure and sense of purpose is critical for moving forward in recovery. Progress is empowering so you want to do all you can to encourage the accomplishment of achievable daily goals.

It's also important that people in recovery learn to better manage difficult emotions that arise from stress or situations that prompt anxiety, fear or loneliness. Prior to treatment, stress and difficult emotions were probably dealt with by numbing out with substances. Now, the person must find new ways to cope. Ongoing counseling and classes that help people with anger or stress management can be excellent outlets for emotion management. Involvement in a 12-step program can also expose the person to individuals who may be willing to sponsor them and provide a personalized level of accountability in their recovery efforts. In the next chapter, we will go into much greater depth about how you, as the recovery director, can help promote self-care in the addiction recovery process.

Managing relapse
If the person does relapse, it should not be viewed as a sign of failure: theirs or yours. Instead, focus your energy on trying to help them get back on track as soon as possible. Reach out and encourage them to start working their recovery program again. They got clean once, they can do it again. You might also encourage the person to contact the center where they received their treatment to see if they offer a refresher course. If available, these usually last 2-4 weeks.

As powerful as the craving cycle can be, it is not beyond their ability to control if the person has a strong support system in place that can give perspective and remind them of what they need to do. For some people a relapse is merely a "slip" that they can quickly correct. For others, it is like falling from a high cliff and they may need treatment again. As a director of recovery, you are not performing an intervention per se when someone relapses but simply trying to facilitate a return to the recovery principles to which the person has been exposed. Ultimately, it is their life and they have to decide whether they'll return to recovery or spiral back into their addiction.

There's a good reason people in recovery try to abide by the saying, "One day at a time." It can be overwhelming to think that you have to remain free from substances for the rest of your life. Relapse is more likely when people lean too far out into the future and start asking all the "what if" questions. Instead, help them focus on making the best decisions they can today. Extend grace and encourage them to learn from their mistakes and remind them that they only really fail if they stop trying.

In chapter 7, we will explore why self-care is a vital part of recovery and how the church can help encourage self-care in a number of different ways.

Works Cited

National Institute of Drug Abuse. (2008, July). Relapse rates for drug addiction are similar to those of other well-characterized chronic illnesses. Retrieved from Addiction Science: From Molecules to Managed Care: www.drugabuse.gov/publications/addiction-science/relapse/relapse-rates-drug-addiction-are-similar-to-those-other-well-characterized-chronic-ill

Polcin, D. L. (2010, June). Sober living houses for alcohol and drug dependence: 18-Month outcomes. Journal of Substance Abuse Treatment, 356–365, June, Volume 38, Issue 4.

Chapter 7: Promoting self-care in addiction recovery

Some people characterize addictive behaviors as selfish. And in one sense they are. Addiction, by its very nature, has an insatiable, misplaced hunger that consumes a person to the extent that they are no longer attentive to the needs of others. All the addict really cares about is satisfying the urgent need for the next "fix." For many, self-destructive behaviors such as using alcohol or other drugs, practicing unsafe sex, gambling, and maintaining poor eating, exercise and sleep habits have become a way of life.

But, when a person gets sober, a whole new world opens up – a world in which they often don't know how to live. One of the more difficult changes for many recovering individuals is the transition from self-destructive behavior to healthy self-care.

I remember a woman, whom I'll call Charlene, who came to our church seeking help for her drug and alcohol addiction. She started using substances in high school to fit in with her peer group. In later years her addiction had become so bad she spent virtually every dollar she made on drugs and booze. By the time we met, her life resembled that of a homeless person living on the street. Her marriage of eight years was over, she lost custody of her two children because she was constantly high and her employer fired her for repeatedly drinking on the job. She was living with and financially dependent on her sister, who was threatening to kick her out of the house because her drug use was attracting unsavory characters to their home. As if that wasn't enough self-sabotage, she was severely overweight, practiced poor personal hygiene and ate mostly junk food.

On the outside, Charlene's life was a mess; on the inside she was unconsciously committed to a pattern of self-condemnation that only fueled her addiction. The worse she felt about herself, the stronger the urge to use substances to ease the emotional pain she carried inside. Charlene was so accustomed to living in a self-destructive manner that her dysfunctional way of living had become "normal" to her.

Let's suppose Charlene eventually got into treatment and started down a path to recovery. While in treatment she would begin to learn how to manage her cravings, relationships and emotions in new ways that don't involve the use of substances. She would also be exposed to self-care principles in treatment, such as healthy eating, good sleep habits and personal hygiene, among others. This would be a good start.

But, once treatment is over and the structured environment and constant support of the treatment staff is no longer available, there is a strong possibility that Charlene could revert back to her old habits. Is she able to continue practicing sound self-care principles in her daily routine? What does she need in order to make self-care a high priority and a core principle of aftercare? What can you as the director of recovery do to help facilitate self-care as part of the aftercare program? That's what I will explore with you in this chapter. You see, self-care is not simply a good idea or a helpful recommendation. It is the foundation for a healthy life and plays a critical role in preventing relapse.

Self-care starts with correctly valuing self

The importance of self-care can't be overstated in the recovery process. It's a barometer for how recovery is progressing and extends to virtually every area of a person's life. As a Christian, I don't think of addiction recovery self-care as simply a checklist of wellness tasks to follow. I see the core issue of self-care as value. From value, all other behaviors flow. More specifically, when a person in recovery is willing to value their life the same way that God values them, there is a strong foundation for change to take place. The key is proportional value; not overvaluing nor undervaluing themselves. The Bible uses the imagery of God as the Potter or Creator and we are the clay; the work of His hands (Isaiah 64:8). Each person has intrinsic worth because they are created in the image of God. Human beings are the only part of

God's creation that is endowed with that unique divine image.

It is critical that we help those struggling with addictions to see that self-care is not simply about practicing better habits. It does involve making better choices but we don't start there. We must help them go deeper to understand that self-care is about valuing themselves the way God values them. He values our bodies, our minds and our choices. He has made us to do good works (Eph. 2:10). God wants us to place a high value on our lives in parallel fashion with how we value others. He tells us to "love our neighbor as ourselves," not once but nine different times in scripture (see chapter 10 for a list of these references).

So, our motive for encouraging self-care as part of the recovery process is primarily to bring the person in line with the actual value they have and creating intrinsic motivation to be a good steward of what God has created. With this cornerstone in place, you can then move forward to help lay other groundwork for a healthy recovery. There are three essential self-care strategies that we will discuss in this chapter.

- Understanding addictive triggers

- Setting and accomplishing goals

- Realigning roles and relational boundaries within families

We'll walk through each one in detail. Let's start with the importance of understanding addictive triggers.

Being proactive in response to addictive triggers

One of the most important self-care principles you can emphasize to recovering addicts is to have a healthy respect for addictive "triggers." Ignoring or minimizing the potency of addictive triggers is one of the easiest ways to erase progress toward recovery, even after extensive treatment. As I mentioned in chapter 6, triggers can be understood as points of vulnerability in the war against relapse. Broadly speaking, addictive triggers can be people, situations, emotions, thoughts, sensations or even perceptions that are associated with the person's former substance use habits. For example, say the person in question had a very stressful day at work (they feel anxious/vulnerable) and as they walk by the liquor aisle in the grocery store they have a strong urge (thought/trigger) to buy alcohol to help ease their anxiety. They didn't go into the store with that intention but once the thought is triggered, it is difficult for the person to let go of it unless they have a plan for how to resist that powerful urge.

Those who are stuck in their addictive ways of seeing the world often do not realize when they encounter these triggers. So the first step is making them aware that addictive triggers are going to occur frequently, especially in the first few months following treatment. A close second step is creating a proactive plan to combat these urges when something triggers them. The three most common relapse triggers are: 1) stress, 2) people or places associated with past addictive behavior, and 3) challenging emotions. Let's look at each of them in greater detail and how you can encourage self-management of them in your aftercare program.

1. Stress
Stress is something that we know when we feel it but it's hard to describe. A simple definition of stress might be: a state of mental or emotional tension. This tension is usually a response to circumstances or situations we perceive as overwhelming or out of our control. As elusive as a definition might be, it is the number one reason for addiction relapse. Whether the source of stress is from work, relationships, financial matters, health or a combination of these, it taxes our physical and emotional reserves. People who have a history of addictive behavior typically have managed their stress by turning to substances to soothe their anxiety or numb their pain. Now that they are in recovery, they must learn new ways to manage the stress they encounter.

For example, a disagreement at home between a father and his teenage son ends in a screaming match with the son leaving the home for most of the night. In the past, the father, who is also a recovering alcoholic, would have managed his anger by downing a few beers and refusing to talk with his son for days as a way to punish him. But, instead of using alcohol to numb the anger and relational tension he feels, the father chooses to initiate a conversation with his son to repair the relationship and take responsibility for his part in the argument. The son may or may not respond well but that is beyond what the father can control. The focus is on learning to manage stress by stepping into the situation instead of avoiding it or using substances to medicate the tense feelings. Once a recovering person learns new skills to manage these emotions, it opens a whole new landscape for how stressful situations can be managed in the future.

Most of the stress people feel overwhelmed by relates to circumstances that they aren't able to control. The feeling of helplessness that results can be a potent trigger for a return to addictive behavior. You want to help the person identify which parts of a given situation they have some measure of control over and focus on being proactive in their response to what they can change.

In addition to recognizing and responding to stress triggers, there are other important ways to manage the effects of stress. These include: scripture reading and meditation, spending time in nature, physical activity (walking, bike riding, swimming, hiking), getting a massage, writing in a journal to make sense of thoughts and emotions, deep breathing exercises, getting adequate sleep and eating healthy foods, among others. It takes time to change a haphazard lifestyle into a deliberate routine that naturally counteracts the daily effects of stress. But, with practice a recovering person can transform from feeling powerless to feeling empowered to make healthy choices as part of daily life.

2. People or places associated with past addictive behavior

A potent addiction trigger for virtually everyone in recovery is social contact with people who use substances. These could be old drinking buddies, drug-using friends, coworkers the person goes out with on the weekends or even family members who don't support the person's recovery. When a person is trying to stay abstinent and prevent relapse, hanging around people who encourage substance use or don't support a person in recovery is dangerous and unwise. Scripture makes this point succinctly by saying "Do not be misled: Bad company corrupts good character" (I Corinthians 15:33). And it is a principle of supreme importance for a person in recovery to keep in mind.

As obvious as this principle of staying clear of substance users may seem to you and many others, it is not always obvious to the person in recovery. It's not unusual for a person to come through treatment with a false sense of confidence that they now have the upper hand on their addiction. Some think that they now can go back to "moderately" using substances. If you observe this mentality in a person, I encourage you to counter it with a loving but firm reminder that complete and sustained abstinence is now the norm. The goal is to learn to live life without the need to depend on substances. That means no use, now or in the future.

Encourage the person in recovery to carefully think about where and when they might encounter substance-using friends and avoid them whenever possible. Of course, they also live in the real world where some contact with these people, such as in work-related situations, may be unavoidable. One good way to safeguard against relapse in these situations is to have someone (for example, a spouse, friend or 12-step sponsor) at the event who keeps the person accountable to their recovery plan.

Another powerful and related type of trigger can come from sensual reminders of the addictive behavior. These sensual triggers might include the smell of a cigarette or marijuana smoke, the sight of people laughing and drinking in a bar or the smell of alcohol. These triggers can occur in live situations or simply through exposure to images seen in the media. While it is wise to avoid as many live situations as possible that might trigger these sensual reminders, it isn't possible to completely avoid all of them. Sometimes it's as simple as leaving the situation or turning off the television. At other times it may be more challenging, but help the person in recovery to form a plan for how to avoid the obvious sensual triggers and respond appropriately when they encounter them.

3. Challenging emotions

People with addictive behaviors typically have a pattern of using substances to disconnect from their true feelings. Instead of allowing themselves to feel sad, afraid, frustrated, lonely or angry in response to routine life situations, they have turned to substances to numb the intensity of their emotion. Though it may help them cope with the emotional discomfort at the moment, they drift further away from real self-awareness when they don't allow their true emotion to be felt.

When these emotions are triggered through a present-day event or the memory of a past event, it can cause a strong urge to return to substances to cope in the familiar way. But, learning to encounter the feelings without numbing them can actually be liberating. It's not only possible but healthy to learn to let sadness, fear, anger, frustration and even loneliness be felt. These feelings won't crush or destroy the person and can be used toward growth. The idea is to help them feel the emotion and then externalize it in some way versus keeping it locked up inside. You can encourage them to journal their emotions, talk them out with a friend or go on a spiritual retreat to deliberately encounter these feelings. You might also suggest professional counseling, if this hasn't already been part of their treatment plan, to enable them to make sense of the tangled emotion with which they are struggling.

Setting and accomplishing goals

Another critical part of self-care for a person in recovery is setting and accomplishing goals. Most people, whether in recovery or not, do not know how to set goals that are likely to be achieved. They begin with sincere intentions that eventually get abandoned because they didn't approach goal-setting with the proper mindset. The repetitive cycle of wanting to change habits but continually falling short gradually weakens a person's resolve to the point where they stop trying. That characterizes the vast majority of people with addictions. They initially think a few tweaks of their schedule will help them stop their use of substances but they fail to realize the compulsive nature of addiction and the strong grip it has on their life.

To break that downward spiral of hopelessness that addiction sets in motion, it is essential that people in recovery approach goal-setting with a new mindset. You want to help them achieve the type of growth they seek. Of course, the first goal is to become abstinent from their addictive behavior. Most of what I've written thus far in the book has focused on that primary goal. But, other life goals that are rooted in the ongoing practice of self-care need to be set and pursued to support a sustained recovery. Here are five key areas of life where goal-setting is essential, along with some suggested topics for setting personalized goals.

- Physical – being active, practicing good hygiene, being attentive to one's appearance, eating and sleeping well, making and keeping doctor's appointments, taking medications as prescribed, making time for recreation/relaxation

- Emotional/mental – being attentive and responsive to feelings, externalizing the emotion vs. holding it in, journaling, counseling, reading for personal growth, allowing others to help and support, meditating

- Relational – being with people who support recovery, making time to nurture the most important relationships, being deliberate about helping others in need

- Occupational – doing work that is satisfying, mentoring young people, developing financial aspirations, expanding business interests

- Spiritual – reading the Bible, going to Bible study, praying, getting involved with church and community service

Every person in recovery should have at least one or two goals in each of these five areas, customized to their particular situation. It's better to have fewer goals that are achieved than have many that never get realized. The most helpful method I've come across to make goals achievable is the SMART approach. SMART is an acronym for:

Specific

Measurable

Attainable

Relevant

Time bound

Many people have some familiarity with the concept of SMART goals. Although these ideas may be common knowledge to many in the people-helping professions, these are not principles that people with addictions practice. By teaching these simple ideas, you can help the person with addictive behavior see that their choices make a difference. In case you're not familiar with these, I'll briefly walk you through the main point behind each step.

Make goals SPECIFIC
Many goals are dead on arrival because they never get specific enough. For example, a person in recovery says they want to build a new network of substance-free friends. That can be a good starting place for setting a goal but if it is ever going to become a reality it has to be more specific. If you were on the

receiving end of someone saying this and wanted to help them be more specific, you could ask the following questions:

Where might you find these new friends? How will you make contact with them? When do you intend to begin?

Let's say the person in recovery answers these questions with the following response:

"I'm going to start attending the singles/career group at church that meets on Friday evenings. I'll attend the first meeting next week."

You can see that there is now a plan in place to jumpstart movement toward achieving the goal.

Vague goals are never acted on because the one setting the goals has no clear plan for the journey; only an end point in mind. When you are specific, you ask questions that answer who, what, where, when and how.

Make goals MEASURABLE

A goal needs to be measurable to assess whether you are making real progress toward accomplishing it. If you applied this to the goal of making new substance-free friends, the person would add more detail to their plan. For example, they intend to meet at least one new person every meeting in an effort to build new friendships. This is a measurable goal because after each meeting it is easy for the person to assess whether they accomplished it.

Make goals ATTAINABLE

This is often where goals go off the track. People in recovery tend to be impulsive and want to see significant change in their life right now. That's good as long as the change they are pursuing is realistic. For example, the person seeking substance-free friends could say that they want to have a dozen new close friends within a month. While that sounds great, it's probably not realistic. It's not typically easy to build a comfortable rapport with lots of people in a short period of time. A more attainable goal in this situation might be to build an ongoing rapport with at least one person within the first month and invite them to a social event (coffee, lunch, a concert, etc.) to get to know them better outside of the church group.

Make goals RELEVANT

When a goal is relevant it is in line with the direction the person wants to take for their recovery, life, career, etc. For a person in recovery, relevant goals always have to consider the consequences of how a particular decision will either strengthen their resolve toward abstinence or weaken it. For example, a person who says they are seeking substance-free friends might have to take a pass on participating in the after-work happy hour with their coworkers because it potentially weakens their resolve toward abstinence. Though they consider some of these people friends and would like to socialize with them, doing so could compromise their recovery efforts. When goals are relevant, they are focused on the larger outcome. If they don't help to fulfill that outcome, they should be revised.

Make goals TIME BOUND

Ideally, all goals should have a deadline. A deadline creates a sense of urgency to continually work on the goal. And you don't only need one deadline. Sometimes it's best to create several mini deadlines to help foster motivation. For example, if the person seeking substance-free friends starts with a deadline of having one new friend in the first month, a second new friend by the second month and a third new friend by the third month, these incremental deadlines are serving the purpose.

Put goals in writing

The physical act of writing down a goal that is SMART makes it real and concrete. Once it is written down, it needs to be reviewed on a regular basis to keep the goal in the front of the person's mind. It's also preferable that the goal is shared with at least one, possibly two, other people who will hold the person accountable for their intended change(s). This person could be a spouse, 12-step sponsor, friend in recovery or other person who is supportive of their recovery efforts.

Incorporating spiritual disciplines into SMART goals
When working with a person I know is already a Christian, I always try to incorporate some spiritual disciplines into the SMART goals to help nurture their relationship with God. For example, I'll encourage goals such as daily Bible reading. A psalm, proverb or a chapter from the gospels each day would be a good start. There are also the Life Recovery Bible in the New Living Translation and the NIV Celebrate Recovery Bible, both of which are designed for the Christian who is seeking God's view on recovery and the non-Christian who is seeking God and answers to recovery.

You could also suggest a good devotional that is specifically targeted to those with addictions, such as One Day at a Time: The Devotional for Overcomers by Neil Anderson, or the Life Recovery Devotional: Thirty Meditations from Scripture for Each Step in Recovery by Stephen Arterburn and David Stoop, or the Celebrate Recovery Daily Devotional by John Baker, Johnny Baker and Mac Owen. All of these resources are described in greater detail in chapter 10.

An invaluable way to help those in recovery internalize biblical principles is to encourage them to memorize short passages of scripture that would strengthen their resolve to resist temptation and avoid relapse. I've provided a starter list of verses that can be specifically applied to addiction recovery in chapter 10.

Another valuable spiritual discipline is to engage in regular times of personal reflection and prayer. Ideally, you would encourage those in recovery to do daily check-ins on their goals, attitudes, behaviors and choices. If the person is working a 12-step program, the 10th step (do an ongoing inventory of your life and admit when you are wrong) can easily be incorporated here on a daily basis. To make this personal reflection meaningful, the person could record their observations in a journal. It could be as simple as writing a paragraph a day reflecting on the day's events and how they responded to each event. Or they could provide a more detailed reflection on each event where they affirm what they did well or acknowledge and problem-solve mistakes they would like to correct moving forward. They could even write out their future goals for improvement as prayers. A longer-range goal might include going on a quarterly overnight or weekend retreat where they do a more extensive inventory on their recovery progress and tweak their goals for the future.

Christian fellowship is another critical element in nurturing the soul of the person in recovery. In addition to attending and worshipping at a local church, the person could find this fellowship through a local Celebrate Recovery ministry. Celebrate Recovery is a Christian-based approach to recovery that takes a biblical perspective on the 12-step program and can be found in many churches across the country. In chapter 10, I've provided a link where you can find the Celebrate Recovery group that is nearest to your location.

Service is an excellent way for the person in recovery to feel purposeful and engage in meaningful interaction with others. This could include getting involved in a ministry within the church, volunteering at a local community agency or attending to the needs of a friend or family member.

These are only a few of the many ways you can help the Christian in recovery practice self-care that will nurture their soul and promote healthful living. But, it is important that you incorporate the principles of the SMART goals even when making spiritual goals. You want these goals to also be Specific, Measurable, Attainable, Relevant, and Time bound to ensure that the person is likely to achieve what they set out to accomplish.

As I mentioned, most people set vague goals and never see them realized. Most people in recovery have tried countless times to stop the addictive behavior only to repeatedly fail. Most feel a deep sense of shame and defeat because they have not been able to turn their best intentions into actionable change. Help them break this discouraging cycle by writing out SMART goals in the personal and spiritual realms and then hold them accountable for what they intend to do. If they make the goals concrete, realistic and attainable for their particular situation, they will accomplish what they set out to do and will feel empowered by their progress.

More consequences of addiction: Mixed-up roles and boundaries
Addictions distort relationships. The substance user, for example, usually takes too little responsibility for their life and behavior while friends and family take on too much responsibility. The relational boundary that typically helps people navigate a healthy relationship is distorted or unclear in families where there is an addictive pattern. What emerges from relationships with poorly defined boundaries is a survival mentality where family members assume various roles to help cope with stress. Though these roles can temporarily lessen stress, they increase confusion and anxiety because the underlying issue of the substance use is never directly addressed.

These roles were first brought to light by Sharon Wegsheider-Cruse in her groundbreaking work called The Family Trap, published in 1976 and referenced countless times, to explain some of the common roles within substance-using families. Some examples of these roles include:

The enabler – an overachiever in the family (often the spouse) who attempts to "help" the substance user by taking on far too much responsibility while exempting the substance user from facing natural consequences.

The hero – the "perfect" child who hopes their exemplary behavior and accomplishments will bring about positive change in the family.

The scapegoat – a family member who draws attention both to himself and away from the addict by creating additional problems through misbehavior, poor grades or even substance use.

The lost child – a family member who appears to ignore the problems going on within the family and finds some degree of refuge by engaging in isolating activities, such as reading books or playing video games.

The mascot – this person attempts to deal with the dysfunction in the family by using humor to mask their pain. This person may crack jokes, minimize the seriousness of the situation or seek attention by appearing as the clown.

Creating new roles and relational boundaries
An essential part of self-care for the person in recovery is retooling their most important relationships with family members and close friends who support their recovery efforts. The term "boundaries" is familiar to most people. But what is not as familiar is how healthy relational boundaries are developed and maintained, especially in families struggling with an addiction.

Relational boundaries in families serve three important purposes.

1. Draw healthy lines of personal responsibility. Think of a relational boundary as a line in the sand. The aim is to assume full responsibility for everything on your side of that line, such as behavior, choices and emotions. Everything on the other side of the line belongs to the other person. You are only responsible for what belongs to you. When there are clear and defined boundary lines between family members, everyone takes full responsibility for their own part in making the family healthy. No one shirks responsibility, enables a family member who wants an easy way out or rescues anyone from poor decisions.

2. Screen out the good from the bad. Healthy relational boundaries

allow good things to pass through while keeping bad things out. When family members treat one another with respect, kindness and care, these gestures of love easily get passed back and forth across the relational line and strengthen the relationship. But, when there is disrespect, harshness or abuse, a firm boundary line that acts like a wall of protection is needed against this type of harmful or destructive behavior. This wall of protection is often what is needed if the person in recovery relapses. That firm boundary sends a clear message that the addictive cycle of behavior will not be tolerated again.

3. Help facilitate healthy communication. Each person in a family should have an equal opportunity to speak and be heard. It's possible to value each member and their contributions even when there is disagreement. In contrast, when one member dominates or withdraws, as often happens in substance-using families, it throws off the balance of healthy family communication. A dominating member shuts down other voices; a reclusive member forces others to guess what they are thinking or feeling.

As you work with families within the church who have addiction issues, you can help them realign their roles and relational boundaries so that each person feels respected and valued. Here are three sound suggestions for facilitating those relationships.

1. Encourage truth-telling
Honesty is often in short supply in homes where there are substance-use issues. Denial, distortion and minimizing are all ways of lying about the real nature of the problem. Encourage members of the family to talk about what they see, hear and feel. Help them to trust their observations versus denying or minimizing them. Families will not be able to build trust with each other if they don't feel they can be honest.

2. Promote relational repair
Conflict is a normal part of family life. But when conflict is not resolved, as is often the case in substance-using homes, it can

linger and accrue in a way that creates negative feelings and relational distance. Promote the biblical principle of keeping short accounts with one another. The Bible says, "Do not let the sun go down while you are still angry" (Ephesians 4:26). Encourage family members to commit to one another that they will not go to bed angry without making a sincere effort to work through any conflict that might be evident between them. Ask each member to take responsibility for their part in the conflict. When conflict is resolved quickly and in a sensitive way, it makes a relationship stronger.

3. Encourage emotional expression
In families with poor boundaries, emotional expression tends toward one of two extremes: either it's largely absent or it's chaotic, loud and hurtful. Neither is helpful nor healthy. Healthy families encourage members to talk about their feelings and respond with empathy and concern. It is through the mutual sharing of emotion that we feel close to others. So, encourage family members to create a forum for the free but respectful expression of emotion, both the easy ones (happiness and excitement) and the more challenging ones (sadness, fear and anger).

Of course, all of the self-care principles discussed in this chapter can be encouraged at any stage in the recovery process, but it is likely to make the most sense during treatment or aftercare. This is because the person in active recovery has gotten some distance from their addictive behavior and can more objectively see the part adequate self-care plays in both healthy living as well as relapse prevention.

Hopefully, you can see that there is only a fine line that exists between what I'm calling self-care and ongoing aftercare. The aftercare program is a more formal process that includes 12-step groups, counseling, skill-building classes, follow-ups/check-ins, alumni services, outings, etc. The three main self-care principles discussed in this chapter (understanding addictive triggers, setting and accomplishing goals, and realigning family roles and relational boundaries) are foundational for ongoing and progressive work in an aftercare program. As head of the recovery ministry for your church, you can have a powerful influence in the lives of those in aftercare by helping them understand and apply the principles discussed in this chapter. It could be the difference between eventual relapse and a life of abstinence.

In the next chapter, we will continue to explore the idea of self-care but focus our attention on what the director of recovery needs to do to stay in physical, emotional and spiritual balance in what is often a very demanding and draining job.

Chapter 8: Self-care for the recovery director

Randall had been the associate pastor of a thriving church for nine years when he was approached by the church board to consider a new position: pastor of congregational care. The church had grown to the point that it needed someone on staff to address the overwhelming number of personal problems that people from the congregation were bringing to staff members. So, they decided to create a position to funnel these issues to one person who would meet with individuals, couples and families up to three times and then, if necessary, refer them to community resources that the church had screened. Randall would not assume the role of an official counselor per se, since he was not formally trained or credentialed for clinical work. But, he would get some additional training in his new role and become the point person for these types of concerns.

For the first few months, he loved the interaction with congregants and felt it was a privilege to be invited into their innermost struggles. But, it wasn't long before the demands from people in the congregation exceeded his availability. Initially, he simply worked more hours to meet this demand. But, it soon became apparent that regardless of how many hours a week he worked, he would never be "caught up." New crises were constantly arising, such as domestic violence, substance abuse, suicide attempts and couples on the verge of divorce, to name just a few.

At about the one-year mark in his new role, Randall was tired, lacking empathy for people and on the verge of burnout. The initial goal of acting as a sounding board and a referral resource for people in the congregation had become an enormous burden. Randall typically worked 50-60 hours a week, but put in immeasurable amounts of additional time and energy each week mulling over the problems and possible interventions for the people he was trying to help. He was physically and emotionally exhausted most of the time and mentally preoccupied and distant toward his wife and children.

The need for self-care

In chapter 7 we discussed how important self-care is for people struggling with addictions to maintain ongoing recovery. It is actually more important for people-helpers of any type, especially anyone assuming the lead role in a recovery ministry, to be vigilant about self-care. Here are four good reasons.

1. Healthy self-care habits equip you for the challenges of addiction work. You must continually draw upon a plentiful reserve of physical, mental and spiritual resources to be an effective people-helper. If you don't continually replenish your own resources and stay fresh, you will find that your ability to help others will gradually diminish.

2. Healthy self-care creates a powerful modeling opportunity. You need to model the type of self-care that you are encouraging people to practice. If you work too much, eat poorly, skip exercise, cheat yourself on sleep, rarely crack open the Bible or pray, how can you, with integrity, tell those struggling with addictions to follow the path of self-care? It is important that you strive for a level of self-care that reflects what you are encouraging others to do.

3. Healthy self-care enables you to have clean, defined relational boundaries. People in ministry occupations are keenly aware that their jobs have blurry parameters around when they should and should not be working. People's needs often don't fit nicely into regularly scheduled work hours. This is true of most people in ministry but especially anyone who assumes the role of recovery director in a church. Crises are a regular part of this job and can occur at any time of the day or night. For example, a spouse goes on a drinking binge, comes home drunk late at night and becomes violent; an adolescent from the congregation overdoses on a drug at a party and is in the emergency room on life support; a woman who is trying to get off prescription meds and is going through withdrawal needs to get into a detox treatment program

immediately and needs help with admission. As director of recovery, it is likely that you would be contacted if any of these situations were to arise with people in your congregation.

4. Healthy self-care enables you to be resilient against stress. Although not every situation is a crisis, there is a never-ending string of demands within a recovery ministry. For this reason, it is critical that the recovery director become vigilant with their own self-care regimen to increase their resiliency to stress and meet the demands of this role.

In the rest of this chapter, I want to specifically address some of the unique challenges someone heading a recovery ministry in a church might encounter and suggest some sound self-care principles to help you face those challenges.

Crisis management and specific types of self-care
Working in a recovery ministry puts you in the middle of more crisis situations than an average pastor might encounter. Crisis infuses a sense of urgency that not only throws your planned agenda off course but can wear you down quickly if you don't have ongoing ways to combat the high levels of stress these situations can create. If you don't make adequate self-care a part of your daily routine, you may eventually experience burnout, which is physical and mental collapse due to overwork and/or stress. In addition to addiction-related concerns, these crises might have layers of other problems that need to be sorted out, such as medical, legal, financial, relationship, employment and housing issues. While the goal is to help people, a recovery director can easily become overly involved and overwhelmed because the needs are often both deep and wide.

Let's start by discussing some practical ways that you can combat this crisis-prone environment with sound self-care principles that address your physical, mental and spiritual needs. While some of what I will say in the following paragraphs may already be familiar to you, it merits mentioning again because it is the application of these principles, not simply knowledge of them that can enable you to manage the demands of your recovery ministry role.

Physical care

I start with physical care because it is the easiest to ignore. In our fast-paced world, we tend to take our bodies for granted because we can neglect them for extended periods of time without much decline. But, neglect your physical needs long enough and you will face consequences. I think of the passage in I Corinthians 6:19-20, which says, "Or do you not know that your body is a temple of the Holy Spirit within you, whom you have from God? You are not your own, for you were bought with a price. So glorify God in your body." We don't worship the body or spend inordinate amounts of time trying to make our bodies perfect, but we are to be good stewards of the body God has given us. Here are three types of physical self-care that will help you do that as you attempt to incorporate them into your daily routine.

Good nutrition. We all know that eating well is a good habit to practice but far fewer people follow this advice. For example, because we are busy, we may often eat on the run, which means eating out or eating highly processed food because these options are quick and convenient. While this practice may be necessary from time to time, it can quickly become the norm if we aren't mindful of what we are doing. There's plenty of good information available online or elsewhere about what to eat, how much and what to avoid. My point here is not to give you specific food guidelines but to encourage mindful eating. Think about what you choose to eat, when, where, how much, how fast, whether it is nourishing or simply fuel. Being thoughtful about your eating habits is a sound self-care practice. Virtually all of the biological and chemical processes that go on in your body, including those in your brain, are created and replenished by the type of food you consume. Make healthy choices most of the time and you will be giving your body what it needs to work optimally.

Sleep. Another important personal habit, and arguably the cornerstone of good health, is sleep. When we have more items on our to-do list than time to accomplish them, we often steal time away from sleep. The National Sleep Foundation recommends that adults get between 7 and 9 hours of shut-eye every night for optimal performance. Unfortunately, many people do not get the recommended number of hours on a regular basis. Again, there are days when unusual demands require that you simply get less sleep than you need. But when these demands continually prompt you to cheat yourself on needed sleep or you have developed bad habits around your sleep routine, you begin to pay the price.

One consequence of sleep deprivation is chronic fatigue. Instead of recognizing fatigue as a sleep problem and correcting it by spending more time in bed, you may be tempted to do what millions of other sleep-deprived individuals do and use any variety of stimulants to keep you going through the day. Caffeine is the stimulant of choice for most people, most commonly found in coffee and energy drinks.

Not only does adequate sleep help you feel more alert but it is perhaps your best defense against stress. Your ability to be resilient or quickly bounce back from stressful situations is much more substantial when you are rested. You think more clearly, your ability to draw upon internal emotional resources (patience, empathy, compassion, etc.) is far greater, and you allow your immune system the opportunity to function optimally when you are rested. Do yourself a big favor and make getting an adequate amount of sleep a high priority.

Physical activity. Again, virtually everyone knows that regular physical activity is a good personal habit to practice but putting that knowledge into action can be a real challenge. A recent study from the Centers for Disease Control estimates that nearly 80% of adult Americans do not get the recommended amount of exercise each week, which potentially puts them at risk for a variety of health problems. One of the biggest reasons that people mention for not incorporating physical activity into their daily routine is a dislike of or inability to engage in vigorous activity. The assumption is that "exercise" means you have to engage in an activity like running, swimming or lifting weights. But, physical activity is more about movement than training. Walking, biking, housecleaning, working in the garden and doing home repairs all get you moving. Regular physical activity is one of the best ways to combat the effects of stress on your body and mind, maintain a healthy body weight, and reduce your risk of many health-related conditions.

Mental care

We also need to be mentally healthy to meet the challenges of addiction-related work. Being mentally healthy requires you to be aware of your thoughts and emotions so that you can accurately monitor how you're managing stressful situations. And it isn't only work-related issues that strain your mental self-care. Personal concerns, such as relationship, financial or health challenges, can add to the stress you feel. The tendency for some individuals is to ignore the fatigue, discouragement, depression or indifference they experience and keep trying to push through it. Yet, these physical and emotional symptoms are signs that something is out of balance. These symptoms need to be acknowledged and attended to. It would be like hearing an annoying noise coming from the engine of your car and assuming it will fix itself if you just drive it more. What happens is the noise gets louder and louder until you have a breakdown. Your body works the same way. Ignore the emotional warning signs and you will end up in a bad place.

When you do attend to your mental and emotional symptoms, perhaps you find that you need time away from work, more recreation or engagement in a favorite hobby or pastime to help clear your mind and get some distance from work. Or maybe you need some professional help to bring your life back into perspective. Many people-helpers are good at giving to others but not so good at allowing others to help them. There's no shame in admitting that you are struggling or overwhelmed or need help. But, the onus is on you to monitor your mental health and take the necessary steps to prevent burnout or feelings of resentment toward the people you are trying to help.

Spiritual care

All of the self-care principles I've discussed thus far are important, but perhaps none are as vital to your overall health and motivation for work in a recovery ministry as your spiritual self-care. Spiritual self-care means different things to different people. To me, it means deriving my purpose for my work from my personal relationship with Jesus Christ. I told the story in chapter 1 about my call to this type of work and why I am passionate about trying to save lives. I don't do this because I think it's a great cause but because I believe it is the specific work God has for me to do in this life. I would be doing it whether I was being paid for it or not. This sense of purpose steers me through those urgent late night calls and the stressful family situations that I'm often helping to solve.

But, to stay balanced, I need more than just my initial calling; I need to be practicing spiritual disciplines on a regular basis. These spiritual disciplines include Bible study, prayer and fellowship with other Christians through the local church. I need to feed my soul by conforming my life and behavior to God's word and I also need the fellowship of other Christians. Given all of the addiction-related problems that a director of recovery encounters, you can't keep your big-picture perspective in balance only by taking care of your body and mind. You also need to care for your soul. I try to take the counsel of scripture literally when it says, "Let the word of Christ dwell in you richly, teaching and admonishing one another in all wisdom, singing psalms and hymns and spiritual songs, with thankfulness in your hearts to

God" (Corinthians 3:16).

In addition to your regular reading of scripture, prayer, meditation, journal writing or fellowship with other Christians, you could also refresh your perspective by taking a spiritual retreat, where you spend a day or two reflecting on what you've been doing, where you want to make changes in your life and how you'll act on those intentions. Doing this once or twice a year is a wonderful way to keep all of your self-care priorities finely tuned and in line with your values.

The need for mentoring, support and accountability

Being the recovery director in a church can seem somewhat lonely at times. You are doing intense work with people on a day-to-day basis, most of it in private consultations, and over time it can feel isolating. Having at least one mentor or a peer support group (preferably one that is familiar with addiction work) that you can discuss personal and professional issues with can be a lifeline. A peer support group could be comprised of pastors, addictions professionals in the community or respected leaders in local 12-step groups, among others. The idea is to have at least a couple, preferably more, people you look to for support, perspective, feedback and wisdom to help you stay grounded in this work. "The way of a fool is right in his own eyes, but a wise man listens to advice" (Proverbs 12:15).

It's also important that you have some established accountability with the immediate pastoral staff of your church so that others are regularly apprised of what you are doing. This not only helps you with accountability but also involves the other church staff in partnering with you to build and expand the recovery ministry.

Another issue related to accountability is the importance of adhering to a professional code of ethics. A code of ethics is a moral code that governs behavior in certain professions. Most professional health and mental health organizations have their own code of ethics, which is designed to act as a set of guidelines for members to follow. Though you may not be a credentialed clinical addiction counselor in your role as director of recovery, and therefore not required to follow a particular code of ethics, it is still advisable that you be familiar with and attempt to adhere to a code of ethics in your interaction with people struggling with addictions. The National Association for Alcoholism and Drug Abuse Counselors (NAADAC) has a good code of ethics to read and follow for your work in a recovery ministry. I've provided a link to this code of ethics in chapter 10. Some of it will not directly apply to non-credentialed people but it will still give you sound guidelines to follow.

Seek out additional training
An essential part of self-care in your role as director of recovery is to continually seek out new training opportunities to expand your knowledge of addictions. The addiction field is growing and it's important that you try to stay current on the latest trends in research and treatment. You don't have to be an expert in all addictive behaviors but you do need to be able to talk the language of addictions and stay current on trends within the field. This will help you both in your interactions with people struggling with addictions and in your discussions with treatment providers. There are many excellent resources that can provide this training through online courses, continuing education seminars and books. To get you started, I've mentioned a few of these resources in chapter 10.

I would also strongly suggest that you look for good training in family systems. I've suggested some online training programs in chapter 10 that focus on addictions and family systems. Addictive behavior in one member of a family always has a strong ripple effect on all members. Family systems approaches to treatment view the family as a unit where all members are taken into consideration. Even if you're not doing actual family counseling, knowing the dynamics of family systems can be very useful when attempting to help families through addiction-related crises.

The importance of healthy boundaries

The term "boundaries" is frequently used but is not always clearly understood. It is a concept that every people-helper needs to understand and practice if you want to avoid burnout.

Think of a relational boundary as a property line. A clearly drawn property line distinguishes where your property starts and stops. Everything that is on your side of that line belongs to you, such as your body, emotions, thoughts, intentions and behaviors. Everything on the other side of the line belongs to that person with whom you are in a relationship. Each person is only responsible for what is on their side of the line; no less and no more. So, if I want you to know what I'm thinking, I need to take responsibility for communicating that to you instead of expecting you to guess. Or, if I get upset with my wife and say harsh things, I need to take responsibility to repair the relational damage my behavior and words have caused instead of simply expecting her to "get over it."

Healthy relationships intuitively respect that boundary line. Neither person tries to cross the line (which indicates an effort to take on too much responsibility) or coerce the other person to their side (which relinquishes responsibility by giving it to the other person). Healthy boundaries resemble a chain-link fence. It has spaces in the boundary that allow good things to pass across the line, such as love, care, tenderness and kindness – things that build a strong, secure relationship. But healthy boundaries also work to screen out harmful things like abuse, ridicule and shame – things that bruise and damage the potential for a secure relationship.

Healthy relational boundaries are rare in people with addictive behaviors. They often have a long history of being in relationship with people who have been willing to repeatedly step over that boundary line and "take care of them" in ways that enable the addiction to continue.

The classic example is the long-suffering wife who is married to a man who is an alcoholic. She has mastered the act of continually stepping over the boundary to relieve her alcoholic husband of any household or parenting responsibilities in exchange for a calmer, less turbulent home existence. Over time, she's learned that when her husband is "bothered" by inconvenient situations at home, such as a two children arguing or a home repair that needs attention, he explodes in a drunken stupor and takes it out on the rest of the family. So, the wife works very hard to make his life as comfortable and stress-free as possible. She does this by taking all of the responsibility for parenting, managing the finances, doing the home repairs, cooking, cleaning, and tending to sick children, among many other tasks.

The husband, in contrast, comes home from work to eat a nicely prepared dinner, settles into his recliner with a cold six-pack and watches television until he falls asleep – every night. To him, this is a nice arrangement. He lives way back from the boundary line because his wife seems willing to step well across the boundary line to manage all of the things he would prefer to opt out of. The wife's willingness to overextend herself on a continual basis sends the unspoken message that she will take care of all these things and he is exempt from those responsibilities. It is a dance that gets repeated over and over until it becomes the norm. It is a very common pattern in homes where there is chronic addictive behavior. In addiction terminology, we call this dance a codependent relationship. Both the husband and wife are unclear of where the boundary line should be and interact in a way that enables the addiction, immaturity, irresponsibility or under-achievement to continue.

So now imagine working in your recovery ministry with that husband and wife just described. In order for you as a people-helper to not get pulled across the relational boundary line and overextend yourself, you must be clear on where that line is and where the division of responsibility lies. For example, you can listen attentively to their story, empathize with their pain, do a screening interview to recommend a treatment path and emotionally support their efforts on that path to recovery. But, you cannot make the husband stop drinking or get into treatment, or rescue the wife from her husband's mistreatment. The couple will have to make decisions that move them toward these changes. You can help them see what those decisions look like and walk along that path with them but not in a way that enables the dysfunctional behavior. In other words, you need to let them take responsibility for the behavioral changes they say they want to make.

Those who work with addictions (including directors of recovery ministries) are often engaged in their own recovery program. That is part of the reason they have entered into this work: they experientially understand the addiction battle and how to fight it and want to use what they've learned to help others. While that can be invaluable life experience for helping others, it also requires the person in recovery to be vigilant about maintaining healthy boundaries in their helping relationships. It is extremely easy to overextend yourself toward people who are accustomed to feeling like they are a victim to circumstances. Here are two specific suggestions to help keep those relational boundaries in place.

- Pose the core question to yourself. Ask yourself: what in this relationship belongs to me and is my responsibility and what belongs to the other person? You should try to be as clear as possible on where that boundary line is and stay on your side. There are certain types of familiar relationships that replicate unhealthy patterns from your past where you might feel the strong pull to cross over the line. But, asking yourself this question can often help you stay grounded and keep the boundary in place.

- Recognize and live within your limitations. Though many people live as if they have no limits, we cannot escape the fact that we live with limits on all sides of our lives. Relationships that are continually pushing against boundary lines may look and feel exciting at first but usually lead to trouble. People who push against boundaries typically don't know where the line is or even if there is a line that needs to be respected. Don't see how close you can come to the edge before you lose your footing. The goal is to live and work within the property lines that define you. If you don't or if you continually flirt with the edge, you will compromise your work with people and eventually go down the path toward burnout.

Beware of compassion fatigue

Closely related to boundary issues is the concept of compassion fatigue, also called secondary trauma. Compassion fatigue is the emotional strain that comes from continually working with people who are suffering the consequences of traumatic events. As you listen to their stories and walk alongside them, you become a witness of their pain, fear and even terror. Over time, this can have a profound effect upon you.

Many of the common issues in addictions work are emotionally heavy: suicide attempts, drug overdose, divorce, wayward children on drugs, financial ruin, incarceration and even death. Add to this the high rate of relapse for people in recovery and an addiction professional can feel emotionally overwhelmed and question whether they are suited for this type of work. When you encounter these and other difficult situations on a regular basis, empathy can begin to wane; compassion is replaced with indifference and burnout is looming if you don't intervene. So what can you do to prevent compassion fatigue?

The best way to prevent compassion fatigue and eventual burnout is to regularly practice the self-care skills mentioned earlier in this chapter: good nutrition, adequate sleep, daily physical activity, managing stress, making time to feed your soul, talking with other people who understand addiction work, and knowing when to take additional time away from intensive people contact. But, in order for these self-care principles to work, you must regularly check in with yourself to assess whether you are living a balanced life. If not, you must take action to correct it as soon as possible. If you find this especially difficult, it might be advisable to seek help from a professional counselor who can identify areas that might be blocking your ability to practice good self-care.

Getting help in the recovery ministry
By now, it should be obvious that if your church embarks on this exciting journey to start a recovery ministry, it will gradually gather so much momentum that one person will not be able to manage all of the work. Despite the challenges it creates, it is a good problem to have. But, you need to have a plan in place before you get to the point of critical mass. Here are some suggestions for how to get started.

1. Gather names of people who show interest in the recovery ministry. Whether you know it or not, you already have people in your congregation who have started their recovery journey. They may not have made it public knowledge, but they are there. Once the recovery ministry in your church has been officially launched, many of these people already in recovery will approach you with their story or give affirmation for the start of the recovery ministry. These are people you want to get to know. These people are your potential hands and feet to grow the recovery ministry. As I mentioned earlier, many of those in recovery want to give back to others struggling to be free of their addictions. Of course, not everyone who comes forth with a recovery story is a candidate to help in the ministry, but you will find some of your best and most committed volunteers among this group. Make time to meet with each person, as time permits, early in your start-up phase so that you can feather some of these people into the work as momentum builds and additional personnel are needed.

2. Identify specific roles that volunteers can assume within the recovery ministry. Some of these roles include:

- taking after-hours calls to determine whether issues need an immediate response or can wait until the next day

- clerical help

- first contact people to set up screening interviews

- identifying leaders for your 12-step programs

Depending on the particular role, there will be various levels of training that may be needed but it is time well-spent. Not only do volunteers free up more of your time as director of recovery but they can help you assemble a committed group of people who have a vision for helping those with addiction issues.

3. Build into the volunteers. The greatest need of your volunteers is to feel that they are valued and appreciated. If they feel that you value them and their contributions to the ministry, you will develop a strong, loyal group that will shoulder a large part of the recovery ministry. Take time to know each person. Also bring them together periodically as a group so that they feel part of a team working toward a common goal.

4. Choose select individuals for advanced roles in the ministry. As you build a committed group of people, certain individuals will emerge who have exceptional communication skills, spiritual maturity, emotional intelligence and wisdom. Groom these people for leadership positions within the ministry. These people, with appropriate training, might be able to deliver training for 12-step leadership groups, write curriculum, do some of the screening interviews, network with potential referral sources in the community, and other important jobs. This is discipleship in action. You are not trying to work yourself out of a job but rather to equip others to expand the ministry.

These are only suggestions that can be modified to fit your particular situation and congregation. But the principles are sound and will work toward building a thriving recovery ministry if you are willing to work through the bumps along the way.

In the next chapter we will put many of the pieces of the puzzle together to see how a recovery ministry can work.

Works Cited

Centers for Disease Control. (n.d.). Exercise or Physical Activity. Retrieved from Centers for Disease Control and Prevention: www.cdc.gov/nchs/fastats/exercise. htm

National Sleep Foundation. (n.d.). How Much Sleep Do We Really Need? Retrieved from National Sleep Foundation: http://sleepfoundation.org/ how-sleep-works/how-much-sleep-do-we-really-need/page/0/1

Chapter 9: Making the recovery ministry work

When I began the recovery ministry at Henderson Hills Baptist Church I knew virtually nothing about how to start and grow a recovery movement in our local church. What I did know is that I was committed to my own recovery and I was passionate about helping others break free from the bondage of their addictions. The rest I learned on the job.

If you begin a recovery ministry in your church, the suggestions in this book will save you hundreds of hours of time and much frustration. But, regardless of how well you plan or how experienced the director of recovery is, there will always be challenges. Many of these challenges will come from people in your congregation because they have misconceptions about addictions and recovery or feel as though a recovery ministry is straying from the core mission of the church, which is to proclaim the gospel.

In this chapter I want to address some of those misconceptions about addiction and recovery and suggest proven ways you can get your congregation's support for a recovery ministry. By the end of this chapter I want to help you see that starting a recovery ministry in your church is not only possible but could be one of the most important decisions facing your faith community.

Common misconceptions about addiction and recovery
Even though it is relatively common for celebrities and other public figures to admit to various addictive behaviors and even enter treatment, people struggling with addictive behavior still face significant social disapproval. Most of this disapproval stems from a poor understanding of addiction and recovery by the general population. The members of your congregation may have a number of misconceptions about addiction and recovery that cause them to resist the idea of starting a recovery ministry in your church. So, it is important that you know what some of these misconceptions are and how you can respond to them in

your effort to educate your congregation.

Here are three common misconceptions about addiction and recovery and the facts that set the record straight.

1. When a person in recovery relapses it means they will be an addict forever.
This misconception is largely based upon witnessing the relapse of friends and family members after starting some type of recovery. For some, a relapse is followed by a rapid return to the former addictive behavior. In these cases it's easy for those closest to the addict to feel discouraged and hopeless that real recovery and enduring change can last.

The chronic nature of addiction means that relapse will often be part of the recovery process. But it is important that we not view relapse as failure and therefore give up on the person struggling with addiction. Effective treatment for addiction requires ongoing attention to the factors that make the person prone to relapse, such as lack of social support or the need for additional lifestyle changes that allow for better self-care and avoidance of known addictive triggers. Though family members may feel discouraged by their loved one's relapse, the person experiencing the relapse is likely feeling an even deeper sense of despair because of their inability to maintain sobriety. They often feel a far more profound depth of defeat than the people supporting them. What they don't need is condemnation or judgment, which will typically push them further into a state of hopelessness. Instead, they need people around them to offer an alternative way of viewing relapse: as an opportunity for growth and to be shown a path back into recovery.

To put this in perspective, if you compare the rates of addiction relapse with other types of chronic conditions, such as diabetes, asthma or hypertension, you will see that relapse, or what in the medical profession is called non-compliance, is proportional to other chronic conditions that are considered difficult and labor-intensive to manage. For example:

- 30 to 50 percent of people with type 1 diabetes fail to stick with their treatment plan.

- 50 to 70 percent of people who suffer from asthma fail to take their medications or make recommended lifestyle changes.

- 50 to 70 percent of people with chronic high blood pressure don't take their hypertension medication as directed.

- 40 to 60 percent of drug addicts will relapse from their plan of treatment (National Institute of Drug Abuse).

You can see that drug addicts have about the same relapse or non-compliance rate as these other chronic conditions. This is not an excuse for relapse but it helps us to respond with greater compassion for the struggle substance abusers face. We also know that long-term drug abuse results in changes in the brain and affects behavior long after a person stops using drugs. I touched on this briefly in chapter 6 when discussing post-acute withdrawal, where the addict might experience anxiety, sudden mood swings, poor motivation, fatigue, confusion, inability to concentrate, obsessive thinking and memory loss from a few months to as long as two years. During the post-acute stage, the risk of relapse is increased. These drug-induced changes in brain function can have many behavioral consequences, including an inability to exert control over the impulse to use drugs despite the consequences. Again, this information is not meant to excuse the relapse but to frame recovery as a very arduous process that doesn't always follow a straight line.

Although relapse is more common than any of us in the recovery profession would like, it doesn't mean that the relapsed person is doomed to a life of addiction. It simply means we have to reframe relapse as a pause on the path to recovery (not failure) and work to help create resilience and positive momentum toward ongoing change.

2. Once a person has been able to sustain recovery for a period of time, their struggle with addiction is over.

When a person enters recovery for their addiction, by all means rejoice and celebrate. But, realize that this is just the starting point. I've known many people over the years that achieved a few months of sobriety and became overly confident in their ability to resist the cravings and temptations that were a part of their addictive pattern. I recall one middle-aged man whom I'll call Darrell. He was a textbook example of how a person can move effectively through the treatment process. He had a severe alcohol and drug addiction and, in an effort to literally save his life, he entered an inpatient treatment program, followed by extended care and from there transitioned into Sober Living for three months. The whole process took him nearly a year to complete. His family was ready to give up on him by the time he finally entered treatment. But, once in treatment, he was a stellar example of how well the system can work for those who are serious about recovery.

The first few months that Darrell was back home with his family he attended daily AA meetings, found a sponsor for accountability, started working with an addiction counselor in his local community and seemed committed to doing whatever was necessary to stay sober. All seemed to be going well. He was eager to get back to work and applied for several jobs, but couldn't find one that paid as well as his former job working at a giant warehouse near his home. Against the advice of his family and counselor, he reapplied at the warehouse and was immediately offered a position at the same pay he was making before he entered treatment. He felt he couldn't turn it down given all of the outstanding bills that had accrued over the past year. He knew there would be old friends at the warehouse who were substance users. But, he was confident that his recovery was rock-solid and his resolve to never go back to a substance-using lifestyle would act as a force-field of sorts and protect him from falling back into that old addictive pattern.

His old "friends" immediately invited him to bars, parties and even tried to give him drugs on the job. For a number of weeks he was able to keep his resolve strong. But, after a few months of persistent coercion by his peers, his force-field started to weaken. It started with going out for a "couple of beers" now and then with the guys after work. He rationalized his decisions as wanting to have a positive influence on the "real" substance abusers, showing them he could stop after a couple of drinks. That led to occasional use of marijuana that slid into some hard drugs at various times. Eight months after he started work at the warehouse, he had completely undone a year of hard recovery work. He was no longer attending AA, had virtually stopped talking with his sponsor, quit counseling and was out with his friends most nights of the week.

How did this happen? Darrell overestimated his ability to stay abstinent and he underestimated how potent the emotional triggers of his past still were in his life. In reality, Darrell stopped working his recovery program in aftercare the moment he decided to take a job in a place where he knew he would be surrounded by people who would constantly threaten his recovery with temptation.

I've seen this scenario play out far too many times in my years of working with people in recovery. People like Darrell don't understand that once a person begins aftercare and integrates back into the flow of daily life, the real challenges of recovery are just beginning. When a person is in residential/inpatient care or extended care, they are in a program with lots of built-in accountability and a structure that keeps them sober. When they leave that structured environment and integrate back into their daily life, they have to deliberately seek out that accountability and make healthy choices that reinforce their recovery. A person is not going to find that type of accountability and encouragement to make healthy choices among other substance users. "Do not be led astray, bad company corrupts good morals" (I Corinthians 15:33).

So, it is a misconception that recovery is complete at a certain point. With time, healthy decisions and responsible accountability, it should get easier to maintain sobriety. But, it is critical that you as recovery director encourage people to think of recovery as an ongoing process. It is a process that doesn't stop with maintaining one's sobriety but extends to helping others in their quest to break free from addiction.

3. Quitting drugs will automatically remedy other life patterns that are problematic.

This misconception about recovery assumes that all of the problems a particular person is having in their life can be blamed on their substance use. In most cases there are clear, connecting lines between the substance issues and other life issues, such as family, financial, personal relationship, and employment problems. But, it is a dangerous assumption to think that once the substance use issues are under control that a person's other life issues will magically be corrected. For example, it is not uncommon for a person with a substance abuse problem to have other addictive behavior (sex, food, cigarettes, gambling, etc.). We need to be aware that addictive behavior can involve more than one area of life. I see this tendency to gloss over the underlying issues in many people from all walks of life, but it is especially prevalent among church-going people. This group tends to want so badly for their loved ones and friends to change that they often have unrealistic expectations for recovery.

A favorite scripture used to justify these unrealistic expectations is 2 Corinthians 5:17. It says: "… if anyone is in Christ, he/she is a new creature; the old things have passed away and new things have come." Now, this passage is referring to the spiritual state of the person. Their old self, the soul that was separated from God before they embraced his death on the cross for their sins, has now become new and is now the lodging place for the Holy Spirit of God. It is a true spiritual transformation that is to be celebrated for all of its marvelous benefits. But, that soul transformation does not automatically mean that a person's ingrained habits, personality traits or idiosyncrasies automatically stop or cease to be issues in this person's life.

For example, a man broken by the many losses that stem from his chronic substance abuse has just entered into a living relationship with Christ. As a result of his new perspective on life, he is finally willing to admit that he needs substance abuse treatment. But, as he gets sober and works on building the skills to stay abstinent, he also sees that many of his old behavioral patterns continue to haunt him. He still overreacts in many situations with anger and control. He puts people down with sarcasm and talks down to people he feels threatened by. He's confused by his lack of behavioral change since becoming a Christian. He was under the impression that it would be automatic.

But the biblical picture of change is developmental and follows a natural progression most of the time. When a farmer plants a crop, he doesn't expect there to be a harvest the next day. Instead, he patiently waits for the natural progression of growth to occur. When a person becomes a Christian, we expect them to grow steadily but slowly in their faith. Maturity, whether physical, emotional or spiritual, takes time to achieve. When a person goes through recovery, we should take the same developmental perspective: slow but steady growth. This keeps us from having unrealistic expectations, allows for grace when there are missteps, and is more likely to feel supportive and loving by the person in recovery.

This is why ongoing counseling should be a part of aftercare. Sitting down on a regular basis with a Christian counselor who is well-acquainted with addiction issues enables the person in recovery to focus on the full spectrum of recovery. This includes not only maintaining abstinence but also managing relationships, money, conflict, uncertainty and self-care, to name just a few.

Helping a congregation understand and embrace a recovery ministry

Some churches are primed and ready to accept the idea of a recovery ministry. They already have the vision for reaching out to those in need and are not intimidated by people suffering from addiction and the accompanying pain it causes. All they really need is a blueprint for how to organize and launch a recovery ministry.

For other churches, the idea of a recovery ministry is scary and is likely to meet with a lot of resistance. These churches need a person who can educate the congregation and staff and help them see the value of reaching out to those with addictive behaviors. In some cases, this educational process may take many months of conversation, focus groups and planning before a decision is made to move forward.

In my travels I have discussed this concept of developing a recovery ministry with many church leaders and an overwhelming number see the need for such a ministry in their church. But getting the congregation on board is often the biggest challenge. The starting point for this education is to expand the church's vision of their core mission: to proclaim the gospel and make disciples. In connecting this core mission with addiction recovery, I think of the scripture passage in Matthew 9:37-38, which says:

"Then Jesus made a circuit of all the towns and villages. He taught in their meeting places, reported kingdom news, and healed their diseased bodies, healed their bruised and hurt lives. When he looked out over the crowds, his heart broke. So confused and aimless they were, like sheep with no shepherd. "What a huge harvest!" he said to his disciples. "How few are the workers! Get on your knees and pray for harvest hands!"

This is the mindset we should strive to have as we think of those struggling with addictions. God has called the church to proclaim the kingdom news and help people heal their bruised and hurt lives. Those who are beset with addictions are among the most bruised, hurt and defeated among us. Because they are so beaten down, they are often incredibly receptive to help; like fruit ripened on the vine, ready to be picked. All many of them need is a loving and compassionate person to come alongside them, instill hope, and point them to where they can get competent help. What better place than the church for this type of love and compassion to be practiced? It is disciple-making at its best. Most churches already have outreach programs in place for various groups of people in need. It is only a small step to extend that outreach to those with addictions.

After you lay out the scriptural basis for a recovery ministry, you would do well to address the nuts and bolts of how the recovery ministry might operate. Many who resist the idea think that developing a recovery ministry implies that the church will become an addiction clinic where people who are homeless, drunk and freaked-out on drugs will be roaming the halls of the church every day. They fear losing their sense of community and the safety they have come to expect in their church.

You can assure them that the ministry is not designed to be an onsite clinic for treating addicts but rather a place where people with addictions are welcome to explore their options for getting help. The ministry is also a resource center, a conduit to community resources for treatment and a place they can find aftercare options such as 12-step groups like Celebrate Recovery. As recovery director you must show them that the ministry is designed in such a way as to not only protect them but give them an opportunity to help. People are much more likely to support a new ministry if they feel they can be involved in shaping the outcome and improving the lives of others.

Approaches to launching the recovery ministry

The approach you take in starting a recovery ministry will depend on how receptive or resistant the congregation is to the idea. You could start small and simply offer one or more 12-step support groups such as AA, NA or Celebrate Recovery in your church. Over time, this would enable you to gradually educate the congregation and expand into a more formal recovery ministry as the benefits of these groups are experienced within the church.

One excellent way to help the congregation expand their awareness of the benefits of 12-step groups is to invite church members who participate in one of the groups to give a testimony of their own recovery experience. This could be done as part of the worship service or at another church event. This exposure helps people to see the redeeming benefits of these groups and plants the idea of how they could reach even more people if they were to expand the church's recovery efforts.

Another type of bridge that we used at Henderson Hills Baptist Church to help educate the congregation and launch the recovery ministry was a series of sermons on understanding the 12-step discipline and how God uses the recovery process to accomplish healing in people's lives. Our senior pastor, Dr. Dennis Newkirk, delivered a series of messages as a way to help the congregation understand the importance of recovery in the life of the church. He wove in biblical stories of broken people, like the prodigal son, the woman caught in adultery or those seeking healing from chronic illness to show how a 12-step approach could help those struggling with addiction and other problems. The 12-step work being done in the addiction field is actually biblically based and groups like Celebrate Recovery are committed to a biblical application of those principles. Having the senior pastor deliver a series of messages like this can be an extremely powerful way to help educate the congregation because through those messages the pastor puts his stamp of approval on the recovery ministry and helps people see the relevance addiction work has to the ministry of the church. Sometimes this is all the congregation needs in order to support a recovery ministry in the church.

You and the church staff can also create a recovery mentality in the flow of daily church life that sends the message to the congregation that people with problems, including those with addictions, are not only welcome but invited to be a vital part of congregation life. I know of churches where the presiding pastor for the worship service welcomes the congregation with a simple statement of empathy. The message differs by the person and church but would go something like this: "On behalf of the staff and members of our church, I want to welcome those of you who may be visiting with us today. We all have a life story and many have painful life stories that stem back to childhood that make it difficult to come to church or trust that church could be a place of healing. If that fits your situation, I want to say thank you for your willingness to come today. It is our hope that you find this a safe place to belong and heal and any of the staff would love to talk more with you if you are comfortable doing so." Not only does this type of welcome create a safe environment for visitors but it also sends a clear message to regular attenders that we are going to be honest about life and the ways we are all scarred and broken – some with addictions and some with other problems. But we are not going to pretend that those problems don't exist. A church that exhibits that type of honesty is one where a recovery ministry will thrive.

Here are some additional suggestions for promoting the recovery ministry at your church:

• Provide educational opportunities through pamphlets, books, videos, or other visual aids for those in the congregation who want to know more about a recovery ministry or who want to volunteer.

• Organize educational seminars with recovery-related themes such as "How to Identify a Substance Use Problem" or "Growing up in a Substance-Using Home."

- Offer recovery-related Sunday school lessons, such as "Identifying Codependent Behaviors" or "Healing the Brokenness of Our Past."

- Develop materials that introduce young people to recovery issues.

You could also join the National Association for Christian Recovery (NACR), an organization that supports recovering Christians and provides valuable tools to help them integrate recovery with faith.

Recruiting volunteers to build the recovery ministry
I firmly believe that if you apply the principles I've discussed in this book you will see exponential growth in the recovery ministry of your church. As that growth occurs, it will quickly become apparent to you that you do not have enough time to do all of the work yourself. This is where volunteers are vital to the success and growth of the recovery ministry. I would suggest that you think through this growth plan before you reach the critical mass juncture so that when you are ready, you can easily mobilize individuals to help manage the increasing demands on your time and resources.

Here are some recommendations for recruiting, training, delegating and reproducing yourself in the recovery ministry.

1. Start gathering people who show interest in the recovery ministry. During the educational phase of starting the recovery ministry, whether that is a sermon series on the 12 steps, focus groups, announcements made at worship, or simply word-of-mouth, people will start to show interest in the work. It's important that a point person (preferably a designated recovery director) be identified from the pulpit during this educational period so that people can know who to talk with about their interest.

Some may be interested in starting their own recovery. Others may have some sort of addiction training background from a former job or class that they would like to utilize. Others may simply want to tell you their story of a loved one's journey with addictions. Regardless, make a point to meet them, write down their name and hear some of their story. Not only does this help you identify potential volunteers for later, but hearing more of their story can also be a screening process to help you decide whether you feel comfortable going back to them to discuss their involvement as a volunteer in the recovery ministry.

When you do find a person who might be a good fit for a future volunteer position, ask them what skills they might be able to contribute. Immediately after meeting with them, make a written notation of whether they are a good candidate for a volunteer and specify which skills they might bring. There is always a need for people to follow up with phone calls and do clerical work. These are time-intensive tasks that are relatively easy to delegate after you train volunteers in the specifics. As recovery director, you want as much of your time as possible to be spent in contact with the people seeking recovery help.

2. Train those who show the greatest potential. When you feel it is time to expand your base for support in the recovery ministry, go back to your notes and choose the people you've met with who made the best impression. Invite them in for a face-to-face conversation to discuss being a volunteer. In the initial stages of developing volunteers it is great if you have people with identifiable skills that can be useful to the ministry. But, even above skills, you are looking for those with a passion for helping those with addictions, along with a servant attitude and a teachable spirit. If you have these qualities in your volunteers, you will have a loyal team that will get the job done. Along the way, some will drop out or show themselves to be less competent at the tasks you assign. But, the best way to build a team of committed volunteers is to regularly show that you value and appreciate them and their

contribution to the recovery ministry. At Henderson Hills we built our volunteer team one family at a time. As we helped families find recovery many naturally wanted to participate in the healing process to help others.

There may eventually be positions that you need help with that require a higher degree of skill, such as doing screening interviews or facilitating a Celebrate Recovery group. These will, of course, involve more direct hands-on mentoring, training and oversight. But, you can usually find a few of these people among your volunteers if you look deeply enough into their character, their faith journey and their skill set.

3. Learn to delegate to grow the ministry. For people like me, delegation can be hard. When I have a great deal of ownership of the ministry that I worked so hard to create, it can be difficult for me to delegate tasks to others, even when I know they can handle them. When you are the recovery director, and everybody wants to talk to you because you are the point person, it can become difficult to know where the boundary line is between truly serving and helping people and overextending yourself.

This is why I've included a chapter on self-care for the recovery director (chapter 8). Part of healthy self-care is knowing where you are weak and where you are strong and allowing people to help you on both fronts. For example, if I am strong in interpersonal relationships, I need to recognize that there could be a tendency to overextend myself in this area because I may be overly confident that I can meet all of the demands for screenings, family meetings, emergencies, etc. I tell myself that no one could do them as well as me. That is simply pride and will eventually lead to a fall of some sort, such as burnout (Proverbs 16:8). So, I need to let others be part of meeting those interpersonal needs, not only to help me but to train and equip others to be more effective in the recovery ministry. On the other hand, if I am weak in clerical matters, for example, but insist on doing them anyway, I risk many things falling through the cracks, and being less effective than I could be. By allowing others to take some of this responsibility I help myself, the ministry and those who find purposefulness in serving the ministry.

4. Multiply yourself through mentoring. Mentoring can be a powerful way to take your experience and learning and pass it on to others. This very scenario happened when I was the recovery director at Henderson Hills Baptist Church. But, it was accomplished long-distance. Through my role as recovery director I became acquainted with a man who lived in Colorado (I live in Oklahoma). He asked if I would mentor him and groom him to become a recovery director. So, for five years I poured much of what I knew into this man. When it was time for me to leave Henderson Hills, the church staff was committed to carrying on the recovery ministry and asked me for suitable candidates. I instantly thought of this man in Colorado. As it turned out, he took my old job and I couldn't have been happier. But, during those years of mentoring him, I wasn't planning for this outcome. Rather, I was simply reproducing my vision and learning in a man who had a similar passion. As recovery director, try to find at least one person that you can mentor in a similar manner to reproduce your experience and learning.

Of course, there are many other facets of leading a volunteer team but these are some key points to be mindful of.

Concluding thoughts
I will close with a challenge. If you've stayed with me to this point in the book, chances are good that you are a candidate for taking on this challenge. But first, let's review the principles we've covered in the preceding chapters:

- Develop a sound, workable model of addiction.

- Designate a recovery director and clearly outline the role and responsibilities of this position.

- Network extensively with local and national addiction resources.

- Develop a streamlined and effective screening process.

- Facilitate recovery through the full continuum of care.

- Promote self-care for those going through addiction recovery.

- Practice your own self-care.

- Educate the congregation, recruit volunteers and mentor individuals to grow the recovery ministry.

So here's the challenge: Take a few weeks to carefully map out how it might look to implement these principles in your congregation. Then, present your plan to the staff and/or board of your church with a general timeline for educating and eventually launching the recovery ministry. Ask them for one year to see if the ministry will take off. Then begin mobilizing your efforts to get the word out from the pulpit, in printed literature and by word-of-mouth. If you are diligent and don't allow the natural obstacles that are common with any new venture to deter you, I can almost guarantee that you will have so many people interested in your recovery ministry that there will be no question of whether to continue it at the one-year mark. The main issue at the one-year point will be how to best manage the growth and increasing needs that are emerging. And, if you gather your potential volunteers along the way, one family at a time, you will be able to plug willing and able people into that growth process who are as passionate about the recovery ministry as you. But, you won't know if I'm right about the potential for explosive growth unless you give it a try.

Jesus said, "Come to Me, all who are weary and heavy-laden and I will give you rest. Take my yoke upon you and learn from Me, for I am gentle and humble in heart, and you will find rest for your souls" (Matthew 11:28-9). The church is the best place for those weary and heavy-laden with addictions to find rest for their souls and begin the life that God intended them to have. I hope you will join me on this journey to see the church become that place of healing for those with addictions.

Works Cited
National Institute of Drug Abuse. (n.d.). Principles of Drug Addiction Treatment: A Research-Based Guide (Third Edition). Retrieved from How effective is drug addiction treatment?: http://www.drugabuse.gov/publications/principles-drug-addiction-treatment-research-based-guide-third-edition/frequently-asked-questions/how-effective-drug-addiction-treatmen

Chapter 10: Resources

The resources listed below are referenced by the chapters in which they are mentioned. Additional addiction resources are listed at the end of the chapter.

Chapter One

Treatment options

Elements Behavioral Health Treatment Programs
This site provides links to the extensive national network of treatment facilities run by Elements Behavioral Health that includes Christian-focused addiction and drug rehabilitation centers that are comprehensive, fully integrated, faith-centered addiction treatment for Christians and spiritual seekers.
www.elementsbehavioralhealth.com/treatment/

The Substance Abuse and Mental Health Services Administration (SAMHSA) treatment locator
A site designed to locate residential, outpatient and hospital inpatient treatment programs for drug addiction and alcoholism throughout the country. You can also access this information by calling 1-800-662-HELP.
www.findtreatment.samhsa.gov

Addiction Treatment Inventory (also mentioned in chapter 4)
The Treatment Research Institute provides a helpful interview document that prompts you with specific question to get an accurate and comprehensive description of the services provided at a given treatment clinic or facility.
www.tresearch.org/wp-content/uploads/2012/09/ATImanual.pdf

Therapist locators

Addiction.com
The searchable directory on Addiction.com includes licensed counselors, therapists and physicians who specialize in treating

addiction and related issues.
www.addiction.com/addiction-specialist/

Psychology Today Therapist Finder
Psychology Today has an extensive listing of therapists in the U.S.
A therapist cannot be listed unless they have a legitimate advanced
degree in their discipline and an up-to-date professional license or
certification. The listings include both secular and Christian
therapists.
therapists.psychologytoday.com/rms/

American Association of Christian Counselors
This organization maintains a national referral network
of state licensed, certified, and/or properly credentialed
Christian counselors.
www.aacc.net/resources/find-a-counselor/

The Association of Addiction Professionals
The site provides a directory of qualified substance
abuse professionals.
www.naadac.org/sap-directory

12-step groups
Here are direct links to some of the most popular 12-step groups.
You can find a helpful meeting finder, which includes both
12-step and 12-step alternative meetings, on Addiction.com.

Celebrate Recovery
Celebrate Recovery is a biblically based approach to recovery that
is currently in more than 20,000 churches around the world.
www.celebraterecovery.com/

Celebrate Recovery® Group Locator
You can locate the nearest Celebrate Recovery® group using
this form.
http://grouplocator.crgroups.info/

Alcoholics Anonymous (AA)
This site provides general information about AA and access to a group locator.
http://www.aa.org/

Narcotics Anonymous (NA)
This site provides general information about NA and access to a group locator.
http://www.na.org/

Sex Addicts Anonymous (SAA)
This site provides general information about SAA.
https://saa-recovery.org/

SAA meeting directory
http://saa-recovery.org/Meetings/

Adult Children of Alcoholics (ACOA)
General information about ACOA and a meeting locator.
www.adultchildren.org/

Self-Management of Addiction Recovery (SMART Recovery)
SMART Recovery is a free and popular self-management addiction recovery approach that applies the latest scientific research to mutual self-help groups and is global in its reach. The first link will provide a general overview of their recovery approach and the second link provides a meeting locator.
www.smartrecovery.org/
www.smartrecovery.org/meetings_db/view/

Chapter Four

Addiction training options

Online training courses for continuing education

The Academy of Addiction Professionals
Offers online addiction counselor certification programs

www.addictionacademy.com/online-class.php
www.addictionacademy.com/programs/courses.php

Fuller Theological Seminary – Certificate in Recovery Ministry
The Certificate in Recovery Ministry is designed for people who
don't have the time or ability to get a full degree but want to
develop a sound understanding and the essential skills for working
with addiction and substance abuse in any type of ministry setting.
http://fuller.edu/academics/school-of-theology/certificates/
certificate-in-recovery-ministry/

Chapter Five

<u>Screening tools</u>

Sample informed consent form for screening purposes
The sample below is only intended as an example of one type of
informed consent. You can modify or change this to suit your
church's needs or expectations.

An informed consent is simply a document that discloses the
purposes, limitations and expectations of the screening process.

What is the purpose of the screening?
The screening is only for referral purposes and not in any way
designed to diagnose or directly treat any condition. We want to
provide you with the best referral and resources available and in
order to make an educated referral, we attempt to gather the
information discussed in the screening appointment.

**What will be done with the information gathered in
the screening?**
All forms and additional information gathered in the screening
process will be held in strict confidence and securely stored. The
information will not be shared with anyone else in the church.
An exception might be a consultation with the screening staff
person's supervisor or one of the church's referring therapists, if
necessary, and only for the stated purpose of finding the best

available referral for that person.

There are legal exceptions to this confidentiality, which include: 1) when the information relates to a clear and present danger of harm to oneself or others; 2) mandated reporting of threats of violence, harm, or abuse and neglect (from evidence or suspicion); and 3) other disclosures that may be required by law. Disclosures will be made to an appropriate authority and will be limited to material directly pertinent to the reduction of that danger.

How long will the screening process last?
Typically the screening process is about one hour.

Is there a fee for the screening?
No. The church is providing this service as a way to help people in our congregation and community find the appropriate resources to begin healing from their addictions.

What happens after the screening process?
After the screening process is complete, you will be given suggested resources that address the primary issues. These resources could include a referral to one or more local therapists, 12-step programs, treatment centers, reading materials, or in-church options.

I HAVE READ AND UNDERSTAND THE INFORMATION EXPLAINED IN THIS DOCUMENT. MY SIGNATURE BELOW INDICATES THAT I GIVE MY FULL AND INFORMED CONSENT TO RECEIVE SCREEENING SERVICES FROM (name of church).

_____
Print Name   Signature   Date

_____
Pastor/Recovery director   Date

Additional Attendees (if applicable)

_____
                                                           Date

_____

Screening inventories

The Multidimensional Addictions and Personality Profile (MAPP)

The MAPP utilizes questions that span a wide range of potential problem areas and can be used to identify any substance use disorder involving common drugs of abuse at any point along the continuum of severity. The MAPP contains 56 questions from four areas typically associated with substance use disorders. The MAPP also utilizes 42 additional questions to identify the possibility of personal adjustment problems or psychological disorders, which must always be investigated fully in order to provide a comprehensive assessment. The MAPP is also available in a computerized format and incorporates a unique referral guide that helps determine appropriate types and levels of care. The MAPP is a well-known, well-respected, and highly reliable test instrument that has been used with hundreds of thousands of

adults and adolescents within various settings for over twenty years. You can obtain 50 screening tests for $88.00.
http://themapptest.com/

Michigan Alcohol Screening Test (MAST)

The MAST is a simple, self-scoring test that helps assess if the person has a drinking problem.
www.integration.samhsa.gov/clinical-practice/sbirt/Mast.pdf

The Suicide Behaviors Questionnaire (SBQ-R)

The brief four-item SBQ-R is a measure of past suicidal thoughts and attempts which have proved to be significant predictors of future suicidality.
www.integration.samhsa.gov/images/res/SBQ.pdf

Stages of Change Model

This site provides a helpful overview of the Stages of Change model.
www.aafp.org/afp/2000/0301/p1409.html

HIPAA Privacy Rule and Local Churches

General Counsel on Finance Administration
www.churchadminpro.com/Articles/HIPAA/HIPAA%20-%20
Privacy%20Rule%20and%20Churches.pdf

Chapter 7

Scripture verses about valuing self as we value others

- Mark 12:31

- Leviticus 19:18

- Matthew 22:36-40

- Romans 13:8-10

- Luke 10:25-37

- Matthew 19:19

- Matthew 22:39

- James 2:8

- Romans 13:9

Suggested Scripture memorization verses about recovery/sobriety
- Psalm 50:15

- Psalm 116

- Mark 8:34-38

- John 3:16-17

- Romans 5:3-5

- Romans 8:30-32

- Romans 13:12-14

- 1 Corinthians 6:12

- 1 Corinthians 10:13

- 2 Corinthians 5:17

- Galatians 5:16-26

- Ephesians 4:17-32

- Ephesians 5:6-11

- Philippians 1:6

- Philippians 3:13-14

- Philippians 4:4-7

- Hebrews 4:15-16

- Hebrews 12:12-15

- James 1:12-15

- James 4:7

- 1 Peter 2:9-10

- 1 Peter 5:10

- 1 John 2:16

Recommended reading

One Day at a Time: The Devotional for Overcomers by Neil Anderson. A daily devotional using Scripture to provide perspective on foundational truths of one's identity in Christ that deals specifically with addictive behaviors.

Life Recovery Devotional: Thirty Meditations from Scripture for Each Step in Recovery by Stephen Arterburn and David Stoop. The book contains 30 inspiring, supportive meditations drawn from Scripture that take you on a devotional journey through each of the 12 steps.

NLT Life Recovery Bible. The popular Life Recovery Bible is now available in the New Living Translation. It is designed for both the Christian who is seeking God's view on recovery and the non-Christian who is seeking God and answers to recovery.

NIV Celebrate Recovery Bible Paperback. This Bible is based on eight recovery principles found in Jesus' Sermon on the Mount and on the underlying Christ-centered twelve steps. Based on the proven and successful Celebrate Recovery program developed by John Baker and Rick Warren, the NIV Celebrate Recovery Bible offers empowerment to rise above your addiction.

Celebrate Recovery Daily Devotional: 365 Devotionals. This devotional is designed as daily reinforcement and encouragement for those on the road to recovery.

Chapter 8

Self-care resources

The Addiction Technology Transfer Center Network provides four self-assessment inventories for addiction professionals to help gauge stress levels, coping methods and compassion fatigue.

www.attcnetwork.org/regcenters/productDocs/2/SelfCare-Guide%20test%20resources.pdf

They also provide a helpful 31-page Self-care guide for addiction professionals
http://attcnetwork.org/userfiles/file/MidAtlantic/SelfCareGuide.pdf

NAADAC/NCC AP Code of Ethics

The National Association for Alcoholism and Drug Abuse Counselors (NAADAC) provides a code of ethics for addiction professionals who are active in counseling, prevention, intervention, treatment, education and research.
www.naadac.org/code-of-ethics

Miscellaneous Addiction Resources

The National Suicide Prevention Lifeline offers more than just suicide prevention. It can also help with a host of other issues, including drug and alcohol abuse, and can connect individuals with a nearby professional. (1-800-273-TALK) or www.suicidepreventionlifeline.org/

The National Alliance on Mental Illness (www.nami.org) and **Mental Health America** (www.mentalhealthamerica.net) are nonprofit, self-help support organizations for patients and families dealing with a variety of mental disorders. Both have state and local affiliates throughout the country and may be especially helpful for people struggling with mental health conditions.

The American Academy of Addiction Psychiatry (aaap.org) **and The American Academy of Child and Adolescent Psychiatry** (aacap.org) each have physician locator tools posted on their websites and resources for families.

Faces & Voices of Recovery (facesandvoicesofrecovery.org) is an advocacy organization for individuals in long-term recovery that strategizes ways to reach out to the medical, public health, criminal justice and other communities to promote and celebrate recovery from addiction to alcohol and other drugs.

The Partnership at Drugfree.org (drugfree.org) provides information and resources on teen drug use and addiction for parents, to help them prevent and intervene in their children's drug use or find treatment for a child who needs it. They offer a toll-free helpline for parents (1-855-378-4373).

The American Society of Addiction Medicine (www.asam.org) is a society of physicians aimed at increasing access to addiction treatment. Their website has a nationwide directory of addiction medicine professionals.

NIDA's National Drug Abuse Treatment Clinical Trials Network (drugabuse.gov/about-nida/organization/cctn/ctn) provides information for those interested in participating in a clinical trial testing a promising substance abuse intervention.

NIDA's DrugPubs Research Dissemination Center (drugpubs.drugabuse.gov) provides booklets, pamphlets, fact sheets, and other informational resources on drugs, drug abuse and treatment.

The National Institute on Alcohol Abuse and Alcoholism (niaaa.nih.gov) provides information on alcohol, alcohol use and treatment of alcohol-related problems (niaaa.nih.gov/search/node/treatment).

48944744R00096

Made in the USA
San Bernardino, CA
09 May 2017